a year of AFGHANS

BOOK 2

LEISURE ARTS, INC.
and
OXMOOR HOUSE, INC.

EDITORIAL STAFF

Vice President and Editor-in-Chief: Anne Van Wagner Childs
Executive Director: Sandra Graham Case
Editorial Director: Susan Frantz Wiles
Publications Director: Carla Bentley
Creative Art Director: Gloria Bearden
Senior Graphics Art Director: Melinda Stout

PRODUCTION
Managing Editor: Joan Gessner Beebe
Technical Writer: Tammy Kreimeyer

EDITORIAL
Managing Editor: Linda L. Trimble
Associate Editor: Darla Burdette Kelsay
Assistant Editors: Tammi Williamson Bradley,
    Terri Leming Davidson, and Robyn Sheffield-Edwards
Copy Editor: Laura Lee Weland

ART
Graphics Art Director: Rhonda Hodge Shelby
Senior Graphics Illustrator: Sonya McFatrich
Graphics Illustrator: Roberta Aulwes
Photography Stylists: Sondra Daniel, Karen Smart Hall,
    Aurora Huston, and Christina Tiano Myers

BUSINESS STAFF

Publisher: Bruce Akin
Vice President, Marketing: Guy A. Crossley
Marketing Manager: Byron L. Taylor
Print Production Manager: Laura Lockhart
Vice President and General Manager:
    Thomas L. Carlisle
Retail Sales Director: Richard Tignor
Vice President, Retail Marketing: Pam Stebbins
Retail Marketing Director: Margaret Sweetin
Retail Customer Services Manager: Carolyn Pruss
General Merchandise Manager: Russ Barnett
Vice President, Finance: Tom Siebenmorgen
Distribution Director: Ed M. Strackbein

A Year of Afghans, Book 2
Published by Leisure Arts, Inc., and Oxmoor House, Inc.

Library of Congress Catalog Number 97-71085
Hardcover ISBN 0-8487-1584-5
Softcover ISBN 1-57486-045-3

*L*ike the unfolding of a new year, this invaluable volume of afghans holds the promise of heartwarming moments, unexpected adventures, and a touch of romance! Here are 52 beautiful afghans to fulfill all your crochet dreams.

As you browse through this annual treasury, radiant color photographs will inspire you to pick up your hook and start crocheting. Our month-by-month format — featuring a selection of wraps reflecting the natural beauty and vibrancy of the seasons — makes it easy to locate the style of wrap that most appeals to you.

The winter months offer an assortment of cold-weather warmers, such as our snowball-inspired blanket, dramatic plaid afghan, and pretty pillowghan — a cover-up that folds into a comfortable pillow. Of course, there are afghans to celebrate the Christmas season, too!

In the spring collections, you'll discover a sweet rainbow for baby, some fanciful floral throws, and an assortment of light-and-lacy lovelies. We also "cover" Easter and St. Patrick's Day!

Our summertime projects include some great throws to take to the seaside, to salute our great country, and to present as special gifts. And for fall, there's a variety of resplendent wraps bathed in golden tones, and so much more!

Even beginning crocheters can enjoy success with our easy-to-follow patterns, step-by-step stitch guides, and handy diagrams. Start making this year special today with A Year of Afghans.

table of contents

RUSTIC LOG CABIN

A contrast in light and dark, this winter warmer brings to mind cold nights spent snuggling under Grandma's cozy quilts. The motifs are patterned after traditional Log Cabin quilt blocks.

Finished Size: 50" x 57"

MATERIALS

Worsted Weight Yarn:

Tan - 13½ ounces,
(380 grams, 850 yards)

Brown - 4½ ounces,
(130 grams, 280 yards)

Maroon - 4 ounces,
(110 grams, 250 yards)

Blue - 3½ ounces,
(100 grams, 220 yards)

Lt Blue - 3½ ounces,
(100 grams, 220 yards)

Green - 7 ounces,
(200 grams, 440 yards)

Lt Green - 7 ounces,
(200 grams, 440 yards)

Crochet hook, size I (5.50 mm) **or** size
needed for gauge

Yarn needle

GAUGE: 13 dc = 4" and 6 rows = 3½"
Each Block = 11" x 12"

BLOCK (Make 20)

With Maroon, ch 7 **loosely**.

Row 1 (Right side)**:** Sc in third ch from hook and in next 4 chs: 5 sc.

Note: Loop a short piece of yarn around any stitch to mark Row 1 as **right** side.

Row 2: Ch 2, turn; skip first sc, sc in next 4 sc and in next ch.

Note: Begin working in rounds.

Rnd 1: Ch 4 **(counts as first tr, now and throughout)**, turn; dc in same st and in next 4 sc, (dc, tr, ch 1, tr, dc) in next ch, skip next ch; working in free loops of beginning ch *(Fig. 29b, page 139)*, (dc, tr, ch 1, tr, dc) in first ch, dc in next 4 chs, (dc, tr, ch 1, tr, dc) in next ch, (dc, tr) in same st as first tr, ch 1; join with slip st to first tr: 24 sts and 4 ch-1 sps.

Rnd 2: Ch 3 **(counts as first dc, now and throughout)**, do **not** turn; dc in next 7 sts, (dc, tr, ch 1, tr, dc) in next ch-1 sp, place marker around last ch-1 made for joining placement, dc in next 4 sts, (dc, tr, ch 1, tr, dc) in next ch-1 sp, dc in next 8 sts, (dc, tr, ch 1, tr, dc) in next ch-1 sp, dc in next 4 sts, (dc, tr, ch 1, tr, dc) in last ch-1 sp; join with slip st to first dc, finish off: 40 sts and 4 ch-1 sps.

Rnd 3: With **wrong** side facing, join Blue with slip st in marked corner ch-1 sp; ch 4, dc in same sp and in each st across to next corner ch-1 sp, † (dc, tr, ch 1, tr, dc) in corner ch-1 sp, dc in each st across to next corner ch-1 sp †, (dc, tr) in corner ch-1 sp, drop Blue, with Lt Blue, YO and draw through, (tr, dc) in same sp, dc in each st across to next corner ch-1 sp, repeat from † to † once, (dc, tr) in same sp as first tr, sc in first tr to form last ch-1 sp: 56 sts and 4 ch-1 sps.

Rnd 4: Ch 4, turn; dc in same sp and in each st across to next corner ch-1 sp, † (dc, tr, ch 1, tr, dc) in corner ch-1 sp, dc in each st across to next corner ch-1 sp †, (dc, tr) in corner ch-1 sp, cut Lt Blue, with Blue, YO and draw through, (tr, dc) in same sp, dc in each st across to next corner ch-1 sp, repeat from † to † once, (dc, tr) in same sp as first tr, ch 1, place marker around last ch-1 made for joining placement; join with slip st to first tr, finish off: 72 sts and 4 ch-1 sps.

Rnds 5 and 6: Repeat Rnds 3 and 4 with Brown and Tan: 104 sts and 4 ch-1 sps.

Rnds 7 and 8: Repeat Rnds 3 and 4 with Green and Lt Green: 136 sts and 4 ch-1 sps.

Continued on page 15.

GARNET FANS

*This gem of a wrap gets its colorful inspiration from
January's birthstone, the garnet. Simple stitches create the
fanciful fans, and a pretty picot edging adds elegance.*

Finished Size: 47" x 64"

MATERIALS
Worsted Weight Yarn:
40 ounces, (1,140 grams, 2,745 yards)
Crochet hook, size I (5.50 mm) **or** size needed
for gauge

GAUGE: In pattern, one repeat and 8 rows = 4³/₄"

Gauge Swatch: 9¹/₂"w x 4³/₄"h
Ch 38 **loosely**.
Work same as Afghan for 8 rows.
Finish off.

STITCH GUIDE

> **TRIPLE TREBLE CROCHET *(abbreviated tr tr)***
> YO 4 times, insert hook in st indicated, YO and pull up a loop
> (6 loops on hook), (YO and draw through 2 loops on hook)
> 5 times *(Figs. 9a & b, page 134)*.
> **PICOT**
> Ch 3, slip st in third ch from hook.

Ch 164 **loosely**.

Row 1: Sc in second ch from hook, ch 3, skip next 2 chs, sc in
next ch, (ch 5, skip next 3 chs, sc in next ch) 3 times, ★ (ch 3,
skip next 2 chs, sc in next ch) twice, (ch 5, skip next 3 chs, sc
in next ch) 3 times; repeat from ★ across to last 3 chs, ch 3,
skip next 2 chs, sc in last ch: 46 sc and 45 sps.

Row 2 (Right side): Ch 3 **(counts as first dc)**, turn; dc in
same st, ch 3, skip next ch-3 sp, sc in next ch-5 sp, 9 dc in next
ch-5 sp, sc in next ch-5 sp, ch 3, ★ skip next ch-3 sp, 3 dc in
next st, ch 3, skip next ch-3 sp, sc in next ch-5 sp, 9 dc in next
ch-5 sp, sc in next ch-5 sp, ch 3; repeat from ★ across to last
ch-3 sp, skip last ch-3 sp, 2 dc in last st: 109 dc.

Row 3: Ch 1, turn; sc in first 2 dc, ch 1, skip next sc, (dc in
next dc, ch 1) 9 times, ★ sc in next 3 dc, ch 1, skip next sc, (dc
in next dc, ch 1) 9 times; repeat from ★ across to last 2 dc, sc
in last 2 dc: 81 dc.

Row 4: Ch 1, turn; sc in first sc, ★ skip next sc and next
ch-1 sp, (dc in next dc and in next ch-1 sp) 4 times, 3 dc in
next dc, (dc in next ch-1 sp and in next dc) 4 times, skip next
ch-1 sp and next sc, sc in next sc; repeat from ★ across:
171 dc.

Row 5: Ch 6 **(counts as first dc plus ch 3)**, turn; ★ † skip
next 4 dc, sc in next dc, ch 5, skip next 2 dc, sc in next dc, ch 5,
skip next 3 dc, sc in next dc, ch 5, skip next 2 dc, sc in next dc,
ch 3, skip next 4 dc, dc in next sc †, ch 3; repeat from ★ 7
times **more**, then repeat from † to † once: 36 sc and 45 sps.

Rows 6-100: Repeat Rows 2-5, 23 times; then repeat Rows 2-4
once **more**.

Row 101: Ch 8 **(counts as first tr tr plus ch 2)**, turn;
★ † skip next 4 dc, tr in next dc, ch 4, skip next 2 dc, sc in next
dc, ch 3, skip next 3 dc, sc in next dc, ch 4, skip next 2 dc, tr in
next dc, ch 2, skip next 4 dc, tr tr in next sc †, ch 2; repeat from
★ 7 times **more**, then repeat from † to † once; do **not**
finish off.

EDGING

Rnd 1: Ch 1, turn; 2 sc in same st, work 153 sc evenly spaced
across to last tr tr, 3 sc in last tr tr; work 209 sc evenly spaced
across end of rows; working in free loops of beginning ch
(Fig. 29b, page 139), 3 sc in ch at base of first sc, work
153 sc evenly spaced across to last ch, 3 sc in last ch; work
209 sc evenly spaced across end of rows, sc in same st as first
sc; join with slip st to first sc: 736 sc.

Rnd 2: Ch 1, do **not** turn; (sc, ch 4) twice in same st, skip next
sc, sc in next sc, (ch 4, skip next sc, sc in next sc) across to
next corner 3-sc group, ★ ch 4, skip next sc, (sc, ch 4) twice in
center sc, skip next sc, sc in next sc, (ch 4, skip next sc, sc in
next sc) across to next corner 3-sc group; repeat from ★ 2
times **more**, ch 2, skip last sc, hdc in first sc to form last
ch-4 sp: 372 ch-4 sps.

Rnd 3: Ch 1, sc in same sp, (ch 4, sc) twice in next corner
ch-4 sp, ★ (ch 4, sc in next ch-4 sp) across to next corner
ch-4 sp, (ch 4, sc) twice in corner ch-4 sp; repeat from ★ 2
times **more**, (ch 4, sc in next ch-4 sp) across, ch 2, hdc in first
sc to form last ch-4 sp: 376 ch-4 sps.

Rnd 4: Ch 1, sc in same sp, ch 2, sc in next ch-4 sp, ch 2, (sc,
ch 4, sc) in next corner ch-4 sp, ★ ch 2, (sc in next ch-4 sp,
ch 2) across to next corner ch-4 sp, (sc, ch 4, sc) in corner
ch-4 sp; repeat from ★ 2 times **more**, ch 2, (sc in next ch-4 sp,
ch 2) across, ch 1, sc in first sc to form last ch-2 sp: 380 sps.

Rnd 5: Ch 6, slip st in third ch from hook, dc in same sp, sc in
next ch-2 sp, ★ (dc, work Picot, dc) in next sp, sc in next
ch-2 sp; repeat from ★ around; join with slip st to third ch of
beginning ch-6, finish off.

SNOWBALL BLANKET

This wintry white wrap is blanketed with plush "snowballs!"
Front post treble stitches contribute texture to the tidy rows,
and a long, flowing fringe resembles falling snow.

Finished Size: 45" x 67"

MATERIALS

Worsted Weight Yarn:
    49 ounces, (1,390 grams, 3,220 yards)
Crochet hook, size H (5.00 mm) **or** size needed
    for gauge

GAUGE: In pattern, 14 sts = 4" and 12 rows = 4¼"

Gauge Swatch: 4¾"w x 5"h
Ch 20 **loosely**.
Work same as Afghan for 14 rows.
Finish off.

STITCH GUIDE

CLUSTER
★ YO, insert hook in sc indicated, YO and pull up a loop, YO and draw through 2 loops on hook; repeat from ★ 3 times **more**, YO and draw through all 5 loops on hook *(Figs. 17a & b, page 136)*. Push Clusters to **right** side.
FRONT POST TREBLE CROCHET (abbreviated FPtr)
YO twice, insert hook from **front** to **back** around post of st indicated, YO and pull up a loop *(Fig. 13, page 135)*, (YO and draw through 2 loops on hook) 3 times. Skip st behind FPtr.

Note: Each row is worked across length of Afghan.

Ch 236 **loosely**.
Row 1: Dc in sixth ch from hook, ★ ch 1, skip next ch, dc in next ch; repeat from ★ across: 116 sps.
Row 2 (Right side): Ch 1, turn; sc in first dc, (sc in next ch and in next dc) across, sc in next 2 chs: 233 sc.
Note: Loop a short piece of yarn around any stitch to mark Row 2 as **right** side.
Row 3: Ch 1, turn; sc in first 2 sc, work Cluster in next sc, (sc in next 3 sc, work Cluster in next sc) across to last 2 sc, sc in last 2 sc: 175 sc and 58 Clusters.
Row 4: Ch 1, turn; sc in each st across: 233 sc.

Row 5: Ch 4 **(counts as first dc plus ch 1, now and throughout)**, turn; skip next sc, dc in next sc, ★ ch 1, skip next sc, dc in next sc; repeat from ★ across: 117 dc and 116 ch-1 sps.
Row 6: Ch 3 **(counts as first dc)**, turn; dc in next ch and in each dc and each ch across: 233 dc.
Row 7: Ch 1, turn; sc in each dc across.
Row 8: Ch 2 **(counts as first hdc, now and throughout)**, turn; work FPtr around dc one row **below** next sc, (dc in next sc, work FPtr around dc one row **below** next sc) across to last sc, hdc in last sc: 116 FPtr.
Row 9: Ch 1, turn; sc in each st across: 233 sc.
Row 10: Ch 2, turn; dc in next sc, (work FPtr around dc one row **below** next sc, dc in next sc) across to last sc, hdc in last sc: 115 FPtr.
Row 11: Ch 1, turn; sc in each st across: 233 sc.
Row 12: Ch 2, turn; work FPtr around dc one row **below** next sc, (dc in next sc, work FPtr around dc one row **below** next sc) across to last sc, hdc in last sc: 116 FPtr.
Row 13: Ch 4, turn; skip next FPtr, dc in next dc, ★ ch 1, skip next FPtr, dc in next st; repeat from ★ across: 117 dc and 116 ch-1 sps.
Row 14: Ch 1, turn; sc in each dc and in each ch across: 233 sc.
Rows 15-125: Repeat Rows 3-14, 9 times; then repeat Rows 3-5 once **more**.
Row 126: Ch 1, turn; slip st in first dc and in next ch-1 sp, ch 1, (slip st in next ch-1 sp, ch 1) across to last ch-1 sp, slip st in last ch-1 sp and in last dc; finish off.

EDGING

With **right** side facing and working across beginning ch, join yarn with slip st in second ch to right of first dc; (slip st in next sp, ch 1) across to last sp, slip st in last sp and in free loop of last ch *(Fig. 29b, page 139)*; finish off.

Holding 4 strands together, add fringe evenly spaced across short edges of Afghan *(Figs. 36b & d, page 142)*.

GRANNY'S MUMS

Like cherished family photographs, this heirloom throw evokes images of bygone days. The granny-style mum motifs are whipstitched together in strips and enhanced with matching ripples.

Finished Size: 45" x 60"

MATERIALS

Worsted Weight Yarn:
- Dk Purple - 4 ounces, (110 grams, 265 yards)
- Med Purple - 6 ounces, (170 grams, 395 yards)
- Purple - 8 ounces, (230 grams, 525 yards)
- Lt Purple - 9 ounces, (260 grams, 590 yards)
- Black - 13 ounces, (370 grams, 855 yards)
- Crochet hook, size I (5.50 mm) **or** size needed for gauge
- Yarn needle

GAUGE: Each Motif = 6¼"
(straight edge to straight edge)

STITCH GUIDE

BEGINNING CLUSTER
Ch 3, ★ YO, insert hook in sp or st indicated, YO and pull up a loop, YO and draw through 2 loops on hook; repeat from ★ once **more**, YO and draw through all 3 loops on hook *(Figs. 17a & b, page 136).*

CLUSTER
★ YO, insert hook in sp or st indicated, YO and pull up a loop, YO and draw through 2 loops on hook; repeat from ★ 2 times **more**, YO and draw through all 4 loops on hook.

MOTIF (Make 46)

With Dk Purple, ch 6; join with slip st to form a ring.

Rnd 1 (Right side)**:** Work beginning Cluster in ring, ch 3, (work Cluster in ring, ch 3) 5 times; join with slip st to top of beginning Cluster, finish off: 6 ch-3 sps.

Note: Loop a short piece of yarn around any stitch to mark Rnd 1 as **right** side.

Rnd 2: With **right** side facing, join Med Purple with slip st in any ch-3 sp; work (beginning Cluster, ch 3, Cluster) in same sp, ch 3, (work Cluster, ch 3) twice in each ch-3 sp around; join with slip st to top of beginning Cluster, finish off: 12 ch-3 sps.

Rnd 3: With **right** side facing, join Purple with slip st in any ch-3 sp; work (beginning Cluster, ch 3, Cluster) in same sp (point made), ch 3, work Cluster in next ch-3 sp, ch 3, ★ work (Cluster, ch 3, Cluster) in next ch-3 sp (point made), ch 3, work Cluster in next ch-3 sp, ch 3; repeat from ★ around; join with slip st to top of beginning Cluster, finish off: 18 ch-3 sps.

Rnd 4: With **right** side facing, join Lt Purple with slip st in ch-3 sp of any point; work (beginning Cluster, ch 3, Cluster) in same sp, ch 3, (work Cluster in next ch-3 sp, ch 3) twice, ★ (work Cluster, ch 3) twice in next ch-3 sp, (work Cluster in next ch-3 sp, ch 3) twice; repeat from ★ around; join with slip st to top of beginning Cluster, finish off: 24 ch-3 sps.

Rnd 5: With **right** side facing, join Black with slip st in ch-3 sp of any point; ch 3 **(counts as first dc, now and throughout)**, (dc, ch 2, 2 dc) in same sp, ch 1, (2 dc in next ch-3 sp, ch 1) 3 times, ★ (2 dc, ch 2, 2 dc) in next ch-3 sp, ch 1, (2 dc in next ch-3 sp, ch 1) 3 times; repeat from ★ around; join with slip st to first dc, finish off: 60 dc and 30 sps.

HALF MOTIF (Make 6)

With Dk Purple, ch 4; join with slip st to form a ring.

Row 1 (Right side)**:** Ch 5 **(counts as first dc plus ch 2)**, work Cluster in ring, (ch 3, work Cluster in ring) twice, ch 2, dc in ring; finish off: 4 sps.

Note: Mark Row 1 as **right** side.

Row 2: With **right** side facing, join Med Purple with slip st in first ch-2 sp; work beginning Cluster in same sp, ch 3, (work Cluster, ch 3) twice in each of next 2 ch-3 sps, work Cluster in last ch-2 sp; finish off: 5 ch-3 sps.

Row 3: With **right** side facing, join Purple with slip st in beginning Cluster; work beginning Cluster in same st, ch 3, work Cluster in next ch-3 sp, ch 3, ★ work (Cluster, ch 3, Cluster) in next ch-3 sp (point made), ch 3, work Cluster in next ch-3 sp, ch 3; repeat from ★ once **more**, work Cluster in last Cluster; finish off: 8 ch-3 sps.

Row 4: With **right** side facing, join Lt Purple with slip st in beginning Cluster; work beginning Cluster in same st, ch 3, (work Cluster in next ch-3 sp, ch 3) twice, ★ (work Cluster, ch 3) twice in next ch-3 sp, (work Cluster in next ch-3 sp, ch 3) twice; repeat from ★ once **more**, work Cluster in last Cluster; finish off: 11 ch-3 sps.

12

Continued on page 14.

Row 5: With **right** side facing, join Black with slip st in beginning Cluster; ch 4 **(counts as first dc plus ch 1, now and throughout)**, 2 dc in same st, ch 1, (2 dc in next ch-3 sp, ch 1) 3 times, ★ (2 dc, ch 2, 2 dc) in next ch-3 sp, ch 1, (2 dc in next ch-3 sp, ch 1) 3 times; repeat from ★ once **more**, (2 dc, ch 1, dc) in last Cluster; finish off: 32 dc and 16 sps.

PANEL A (Make 3)
STRIP

Each Strip is assembled by joining 7 Motifs into one horizontal Strip.

Using Black and working through both loops, whipstitch Motifs together *(Fig. 35b, page 141)*, beginning in first dc to left of first corner ch-2 sp and ending in last dc before next corner ch-2 sp.

Join remaining Motifs in the same manner.

RIPPLE

Row 1: With **right** side facing and working across long edge of Strip, join Black with slip st in third ch-2 sp to right of first joining; ch 3, (2 dc in next ch-1 sp, ch 1) 4 times, (2 dc, ch 2, 2 dc) in next ch-2 sp, ch 1, (2 dc in next ch-1 sp, ch 1) 4 times, ★ dc in next 2 ch-2 sps, ch 1, (2 dc in next ch-1 sp, ch 1) 4 times, (2 dc, ch 2, 2 dc) in next ch-2 sp, ch 1, (2 dc in next ch-1 sp, ch 1) 4 times; repeat from ★ 5 times **more**, dc in next ch-2 sp; finish off: 154 dc.

Row 2: With **wrong** side facing, join Dk Purple with slip st in first dc; ch 3, skip first ch-1 sp, (2 dc in next ch-1 sp, ch 1) 4 times, (2 dc, ch 2, 2 dc) in next ch-2 sp, ch 1, (2 dc in next ch-1 sp, ch 1) 4 times, ★ dc in next 2 ch-1 sps, ch 1, (2 dc in next ch-1 sp, ch 1) 4 times, (2 dc, ch 2, 2 dc) in next ch-2 sp, ch 1, (2 dc in next ch-1 sp, ch 1) 4 times; repeat from ★ across to last 3 dc, skip next 2 dc, dc in last dc; finish off.

Row 3: With **right** side facing, join Med Purple with slip st in first dc; ch 3, skip first ch-1 sp, (2 dc in next ch-1 sp, ch 1) 4 times, (2 dc, ch 2, 2 dc) in next ch-2 sp, ch 1, (2 dc in next ch-1 sp, ch 1) 4 times, ★ dc in next 2 ch-1 sps, ch 1, (2 dc in next ch-1 sp, ch 1) 4 times, (2 dc, ch 2, 2 dc) in next ch-2 sp, ch 1, (2 dc in next ch-1 sp, ch 1) 4 times; repeat from ★ across to last 3 dc, skip next 2 dc, dc in last dc; finish off.

Row 4: With Purple, repeat Row 2.

Row 5: With Lt Purple, repeat Row 3.

Row 6: With Black, repeat Row 2.

PANEL B (Make 3)
STRIP

Each Strip is assembled by whipstitching 6 Motifs together in same manner as before, forming one horizontal Strip; whipstitch one Half Motif to each end.

RIPPLE

Row 1: With **right** side facing and working across long edge of Strip, join Black with slip st in first ch-1 sp; ch 4, 2 dc in same sp, ch 1, (2 dc in next ch-1 sp, ch 1) 4 times, dc in next 2 ch-2 sps, ch 1, (2 dc in next ch-1 sp, ch 1) 4 times, ★ (2 dc, ch 2, 2 dc) in next ch-2 sp, ch 1, (2 dc in next ch-1 sp, ch 1) 4 times, dc in next 2 ch-2 sps, ch 1, (2 dc in next ch-1 sp, ch 1) 4 times; repeat from ★ across to last ch-1 sp, (2 dc, ch 1, dc) in last ch-1 sp; finish off: 156 dc.

Row 2: With **wrong** side facing, join Dk Purple with slip st in first ch-1 sp; ch 4, 2 dc in same sp, ch 1, (2 dc in next ch-1 sp, ch 1) 4 times, dc in next 2 ch-1 sps, ch 1, (2 dc in next ch-1 sp, ch 1) 4 times, ★ (2 dc, ch 2, 2 dc) in next ch-2 sp, ch 1, (2 dc in next ch-1 sp, ch 1) 4 times, dc in next 2 ch-1 sps, ch 1, (2 dc in next ch-1 sp, ch 1) 4 times; repeat from ★ across to last ch-1 sp, (2 dc, ch 1, dc) in last ch-1 sp; finish off.

Row 3: With **right** side facing, join Med Purple with slip st in first ch-1 sp; ch 4, 2 dc in same sp, ch 1, (2 dc in next ch-1 sp, ch 1) 4 times, dc in next 2 ch-1 sps, ch 1, (2 dc in next ch-1 sp, ch 1) 4 times, ★ (2 dc, ch 2, 2 dc) in next ch-2 sp, ch 1, (2 dc in next ch-1 sp, ch 1) 4 times, dc in next 2 ch-1 sps, ch 1, (2 dc in next ch-1 sp, ch 1) 4 times; repeat from ★ across to last ch-1 sp, (2 dc, ch 1, dc) in last ch-1 sp; finish off.

Row 4: With Purple, repeat Row 2.

Row 5: With Lt Purple, repeat Row 3.

Row 6: With Black, repeat Row 2.

LAST STRIP

Whipstitch remaining Motifs together in same manner as before, forming one horizontal Strip; do **not** work Ripple.

ASSEMBLY

Join Panels by whipstitching Ripple to Strip, alternating Panel A and Panel B.
Whipstitch Last Strip to Ripple of last Panel B.

EDGING

With **right** side facing, join Black with slip st in second ch-2 sp to right of last Motif joining at top right corner; ch 3, (dc, ch 2, 2 dc) in same sp, † ch 1, (2 dc in next ch-1 sp, ch 1) 4 times, ★ dc in next 2 ch-2 sps, ch 1, (2 dc in next ch-1 sp, ch 1) 4 times, (2 dc, ch 2, 2 dc) in next ch-2 sp, ch 1, (2 dc in next ch-1 sp, ch 1) 4 times; repeat from ★ 5 times **more**, (2 dc, ch 2, 2 dc) in next ch-2 sp, ch 1; (2 dc, ch 1) evenly spaced across to next ch-2 sp, (2 dc, ch 2, 2 dc) in ch-2 sp, ch 1, (2 dc in next ch-1 sp, ch 1) 4 times †, (2 dc, ch 2, 2 dc) in next ch-2 sp, repeat from † to † once; join with slip st to first dc, finish off.

RUSTIC LOG CABIN Continued from page 6.

Rnd 9: With **right** side facing, join Tan with slip st in marked corner ch-1 sp; ch 4, dc in same sp and in each st across to next corner ch-1 sp, ★ (dc, tr, ch 1, tr, dc) in corner ch-1 sp, dc in each st across to next corner ch-1 sp; repeat from ★ around, (dc, tr) in same sp as first tr, ch 1; join with slip st to first tr, finish off.

ASSEMBLY

Using Placement Diagram as a guide for color position, place two Blocks with **wrong** sides together. Using Tan and working through inside loops only, whipstitch Blocks together *(Fig. 35a, page 141)*, forming 4 vertical strips of 5 Blocks each, beginning in first corner ch and ending in next corner ch; whipstitch strips together in same manner.

EDGING

With **right** side facing, join Tan with slip st in any corner ch-1 sp; ch 3, dc in next tr and in each st, sp, and joining across to next corner ch-1 sp, ★ (dc, ch 1, dc) in corner ch-1 sp, dc in each st, sp, and joining across to next corner ch-1 sp; repeat from ★ around, dc in same sp as first dc, ch 1; join with slip st to first dc, finish off.

PLACEMENT DIAGRAM

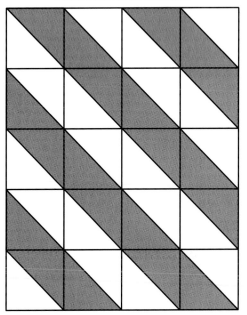

VICTORIAN GEM

This captivating cover-up shines with quiet elegance. The hexagonal motifs get their faceted gemstone look by working alternate rounds of front and back post double crochets.

Finished Size: 46" x 61"

MATERIALS

Worsted Weight Yarn:
Ecru - 39^1/$_2$ ounces,
(1,120 grams, 2,710 yards)
Lt Rose - 4 ounces,
(110 grams, 275 yards)
Rose - 7 ounces,
(200 grams, 480 yards)
Dk Rose - 12^1/$_2$ ounces,
(360 grams, 855 yards)
Crochet hook, size J (6.00 mm) **or** size
needed for gauge
Yarn needle

GAUGE: Rnds 1-3 = 3^1/$_2$"
(from point to point)
Each Motif = 7^1/$_4$"
(from point to point)

STITCH GUIDE

**FRONT POST DOUBLE CROCHET
(abbreviated FPdc)**
YO, insert hook from **front** to **back** around post of st indicated, YO and pull up a loop *(Fig. 12, page 135)*, (YO and draw through 2 loops on hook) twice **(counts as one dc)**.

BACK POST DOUBLE CROCHET *(abbreviated BPdc)*
YO, insert hook from **back** to **front** around post of st indicated, YO and pull up a loop *(Fig. 15, page 136)*, (YO and draw through 2 loops on hook) twice **(counts as one dc)**.

MOTIF (Make 72)

With Ecru, ch 4; join with slip st to form a ring.

Rnd 1 (Right side)**:** Ch 3 **(counts as first dc)**, dc in ring, ch 1, (2 dc in ring, ch 1) 5 times; join with slip st to first dc, finish off: 12 dc.

Note: Loop a short piece of yarn around any stitch to mark Rnd 1 as **right** side.

Rnd 2: With **right** side facing, join Lt Rose with slip st in any ch-1 sp; ch 4 **(counts as first dc plus ch 1, now and throughout)**, dc in same sp, work FPdc around next 2 dc, ★ (dc, ch 1, dc) in next ch-1 sp, work FPdc around next 2 dc; repeat from ★ around; join with slip st to first dc, finish off: 24 dc.

Rnd 3: With **right** side facing, join Ecru with slip st in any ch-1 sp; ch 4, dc in same sp, work BPdc around next 4 dc, ★ (dc, ch 1, dc) in next ch-1 sp, work BPdc around next 4 dc; repeat from ★ around; join with slip st to first dc, finish off: 36 dc.

Rnd 4: With **right** side facing, join Rose with slip st in any ch-1 sp; ch 4, dc in same sp, work FPdc around next 6 dc, ★ (dc, ch 1, dc) in next ch-1 sp, work FPdc around next 6 dc; repeat from ★ around; join with slip st to first dc, finish off: 48 dc.

Rnd 5: With **right** side facing, join Ecru with slip st in any ch-1 sp; ch 4, dc in same sp, work BPdc around next 8 dc, ★ (dc, ch 1, dc) in next ch-1 sp, work BPdc around next 8 dc; repeat from ★ around; join with slip st to first dc, finish off: 60 dc.

Continued on page 25.

PRETTY PILLOWGHAN

This pretty cover-up is full of surprises! When it's unfolded, a pocket created with a four-square block keeps your feet toasty. Once you've warmed up, you can fold the wrap into the pocket to create a soft, comfortable pillow. You'll love its two-in-one simplicity!

Finished Size: 37" x 55"

MATERIALS
Worsted Weight Yarn:
Ecru - 27 ounces, (770 grams, 1,525 yards)
Dk Rose - 10 ounces, (280 grams, 565 yards)
Pink - 6 ounces, (170 grams, 340 yards)
Crochet hooks, sizes K (6.50 mm) **and** Q (15.00 mm) **or** sizes needed for gauge

GAUGE: With smaller size hook and one stand of yarn,
6 dc = 2"
With larger size hook and two strands of yarn,
8 dc = 5"
Each Square = 9"

SQUARE (Make 28)
With small size hook and one strand of Pink, ch 5; join with slip st to form a ring.
Rnd 1: Ch 3 **(counts as first dc, now and throughout)**, 2 dc in ring, loop a short piece of yarn around center dc to mark **right** side, ch 3, **turn**; dc in first dc, 2 dc in each of next 2 dc, ch 3, **turn**; ★ with ch-3 **behind** group just made, 3 dc in ring, ch 3, **turn**; dc in first dc, 2 dc in each of next 2 dc, ch 3, **turn**; repeat from ★ 6 times **more**; join with slip st to first dc, finish off: 8 Petals.
Rnd 2: With **right** side facing and large size hook, join 2 strands of Dk Rose with slip st in any ch-3 sp; ch 3, (2 dc, ch 2, 2 dc) in next ch-3 sp, ★ dc in next ch-3 sp, (2 dc, ch 2, 2 dc) in next ch-3 sp; repeat from ★ around; join with slip st to first dc, finish off: 20 dc.
Rnd 3: With **right** side facing and large size hook, join 2 stands of Ecru with slip st in any ch-2 sp; ch 3, (dc, ch 2, 2 dc) in same sp, dc in next 5 dc, ★ (2 dc, ch 2, 2 dc) in next ch-2 sp, dc in next 5 dc; repeat from ★ around; join with slip st to first dc: 36 dc.
Rnd 4: Ch 3, dc in next dc, (2 dc, ch 2, 2 dc) in next ch-2 sp, ★ dc in next 9 dc, (2 dc, ch 2, 2 dc) in next ch-2 sp; repeat from ★ 2 times **more**, dc in last 7 dc; join with slip st to first dc, finish off: 52 dc.

ASSEMBLY
For Afghan, using 2 strands of Ecru and working through inside loops only, whipstitch Squares together **(Fig. 35a, page 141)**, forming 4 vertical Strips of 6 Squares each, beginning in second ch of first corner ch-2 and ending in first ch of next corner ch-2; whipstitch strips together in same manner.

For pocket, whipstitch remaining Squares together, forming 2 vertical strips of 2 squares each; whipstitch strips together in same manner.

EDGING
With **right** side of Afghan facing and large size hook, join 2 strands of Ecru with slip st in bottom left corner ch-2 sp; ch 1, 3 sc in same sp, sc in each dc across to first ch-sp, sc in ch-sp and in next joining, to attach bottom of pocket to Afghan, place **right** side of pocket against next 2 Squares on **wrong** side of Afghan; working through **both** thicknesses, sc in each ch-sp and each dc across pocket, sc in each dc, ch-sp, and joining around working 3 sc in each corner ch-2 sp; join with slip st to first sc, finish off.

Sew sides of pocket to Afghan, leaving top edge free.

FOLDING INSTRUCTIONS
Lay Afghan on flat surface with **right** side facing (grey area on Fig. 1 indicates pocket). Fold outside strips over inside strips **(Fig. 1)**, then fold 4 Squares down, twice. Turn pocket over folded Afghan to form pillow.

Fig. 1

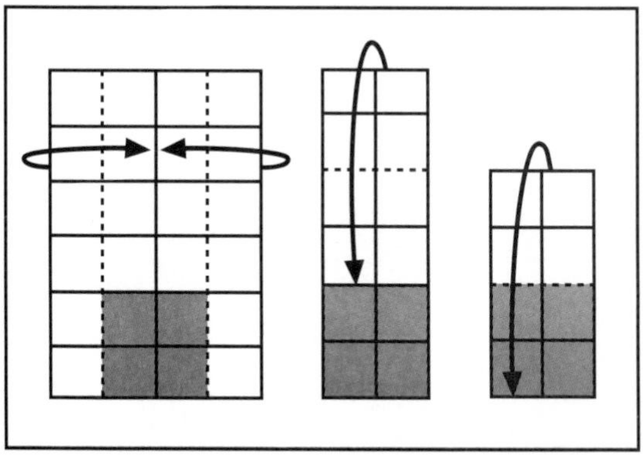

VALENTINE WRAP

Embellished with pretty popcorn hearts, this romantic wrap is fashioned in red for Valentine's Day. The soft, cozy afghan is worked in panels using a Q hook and two strands of brushed acrylic yarn.

Finished Size: 54" x 76"

MATERIALS
Worsted Weight Brushed Acrylic Yarn:
58 ounces, (1,650 grams, 4,475 yards)
Crochet hook, size Q (15.00 mm)

GAUGE: In pattern, 7 sc and 8 rows = 4"

Gauge Swatch: 4"
Ch 8 **loosely**.
Work same as Afghan for 8 rows.
Finish off.

STITCH GUIDE

LONG SINGLE CROCHET (abbreviated LSC)
Sc **loosely** in free loop of sc *(Fig. 29a, page 139)* one row **below** next sc *(Fig. 20, page 137)* **(counts as one sc)**.
POPCORN
(Sc, dc, sc) in Front Loop Only of next sc, drop loop from hook, insert hook in first sc of 3-st group, hook dropped loop and draw through. Push Popcorn to **right** side.

Note: Entire Afghan is worked holding two strands of yarn together.

PANEL (Make 3)
CENTER
Ch 24 **loosely**.
Row 1 (Right side)**:** Sc in second ch from hook and in each ch across: 23 sc.
Note: Loop a short piece of yarn around any stitch to mark Row 1 as **right** side and bottom edge.
Row 2: Ch 1, turn; working in Front Loops Only *(Fig. 28, page 139)*, sc in each sc across.
Row 3: Ch 1, turn; sc in Back Loop Only of first sc, ★ work LSC, sc in Back Loop Only of next sc; repeat from ★ across.
Row 3: Ch 1, turn; sc in Back Loop Only of first sc, ★ work LSC, sc in Back Loop Only of next sc; repeat from ★ across.
Row 4: Ch 1, turn; sc in Front Loop Only of each sc across.
Row 5: Ch 1, turn; sc in Back Loop Only of first sc, ★ work LSC, sc in Back Loop Only of next sc; repeat from ★ across.
Rows 6-9: Repeat Rows 4 and 5 twice.

Row 10: Ch 1, turn; working in Front Loops Only, sc in first 11 sc, work Popcorn, sc in last 11 sc: 22 sc and one Popcorn.
Row 11: Ch 1, turn; sc in Back Loop Only of first sc, work LSC, (sc in Back Loop Only of next sc, work LSC) 4 times, sc in Back Loop Only of next 3 sts, (work LSC, sc in Back Loop Only of next sc) across: 23 sc.
Row 12: Ch 1, turn; working in Front Loops Only, sc in first 9 sc, work Popcorn, sc in next 3 sc, work Popcorn, sc in last 9 sc: 21 sc and 2 Popcorns.
Row 13: Ch 1, turn; sc in Back Loop Only of first sc, (work LSC, sc in Back Loop Only of next sc) 3 times, (work LSC, sc in Back Loop Only of next 3 sts) twice, (work LSC, sc in Back Loop Only of next sc) across: 23 sc.
Row 14: Ch 1, turn; working in Front Loops Only, sc in first 7 sc, (work Popcorn, sc in next 7 sc) twice: 21 sc and 2 Popcorns.
Row 15: Ch 1, turn; sc in Back Loop Only of first sc, work LSC, (sc in Back Loop Only of next sc, work LSC) twice, ★ sc in Back Loop Only of next 3 sts, work LSC, (sc in Back Loop Only of next sc, work LSC) twice; repeat from ★ once **more**, sc in Back Loop Only of last sc: 23 sc.
Row 16: Ch 1, turn; working in Front Loops Only, sc in first 5 sc, (work Popcorn, sc in next 5 sc) 3 times: 20 sc and 3 Popcorns.
Row 17: Ch 1, turn; sc in Back Loop Only of first sc, work LSC, sc in Back Loop Only of next sc, work LSC, ★ sc in Back Loop Only of next 3 sts, work LSC, sc in Back Loop Only of next sc, work LSC; repeat from ★ across to last sc, sc in Back Loop Only of last sc: 23 sc.
Row 18 and 19: Repeat Rows 16 and 17.
Row 20: Ch 1, turn; working Front Loops Only, sc in first 7 sc, work Popcorn, sc in next sc, work Popcorn, sc in next 3 sc, work Popcorn, sc in next sc, work Popcorn, sc in last 7 sc: 19 sc and 4 Popcorns.
Row 21: Ch 1, turn; sc in Back Loop Only of first sc, work LSC, (sc in Back Loop Only of next sc, work LSC) twice, sc in Back Loop Only of next 5 sts, work LSC, sc in Back Loop Only of next 5 sts, (work LSC, sc in Back Loop Only of next sc) across: 23 sc.
Rows 22-31: Repeat Rows 4 and 5, 5 times.
Rows 32-141: Repeat Rows 10-31, 5 times.
Do **not** finish off.

Continued on page 25.

CHAIN OF HEARTS

Love abounds on this precious throw, which features chains of hearts in alternating shades of soft blue. A lacy border finishes each strip.

Finished Size: 58" x 69"

MATERIALS

Worsted Weight Yarn:
  Ecru - 21 ounces, (600 grams, 1,560 yards)
  Blue - 17 ounces, (480 grams, 1,265 yards)
  Lt Blue - 9 ounces, (260 grams, 670 yards)
Crochet hook, size H (5.00 mm) **or** size needed
  for gauge
Yarn needle

GAUGE: 16 sc and 18 rows = 4"
        Each Strip = 8¹/₄" wide

STITCH GUIDE

> **DECREASE** (uses next 2 sc)
> ★ YO, insert hook in **next** sc, YO and pull up a loop, YO and draw through 2 loops on hook; repeat from ★ once **more**, YO and draw through all 3 loops on hook (**counts as one dc**).

STRIP A (Make 4)
CENTER
HEART COLOR SEQUENCE
Work one Heart **each** in the following colors: Blue, (Lt Blue, Blue) 10 times.
FIRST HEART
Row 1: With Blue, ch 2, 3 sc in second ch from hook: 3 sc.
Row 2 (Right side)**:** Ch 1, turn; 2 sc in first sc, sc in last 2 sc: 4 sc.
Note: Loop a short piece of yarn around any stitch to mark Row 2 as **right** side and bottom edge.
Rows 3-9: Ch 1, turn; 2 sc in first sc, sc in next sc and in each sc across: 11 sc.
Row 10: Ch 2, turn; dc in next 4 sc, slip st in next sc, dc in next 3 sc, decrease: 8 dc.

Edging Rnd: Ch 1, do **not** turn; working in end of rows, 2 sc in first row, sc in last 9 rows; (sc, ch 1, sc) in free loop of beginning ch at base of first sc *(Fig. 29b, page 139)*, place marker around last sc made for st placement; working in end of rows, sc in first 9 rows, 2 sc in last row; sc in first dc on Row 10, 2 dc in each of next 2 dc, sc in next dc, slip st in next slip st, sc in next dc, 2 dc in each of next 2 dc, sc in last dc; join with slip st to first sc, finish off: 36 sts.

REMAINING 20 HEARTS
Row 1: With **wrong** side of **previous** Heart facing, join next color with slip st in slip st at center top of Edging Rnd; ch 1, 3 sc in same st: 3 sc.
Row 2 (Right side): Ch 1, turn; 2 sc in first sc, sc in last 2 sc: 4 sc.
Rows 3-10: Work same as First Heart: 8 dc.
Edging Rnd: Ch 1, do **not** turn; working in end of rows, 2 sc in first row, sc in last 9 rows; sc in same st as joining of Row 1, ch 1, working along opposite side of Heart, sc in same st as joining of Row 1; working in end of rows, sc in first 4 rows, place marker around last sc made for st placement, sc in next 5 rows, 2 sc in last row; sc in first dc on Row 10, 2 dc in each of next 2 dc, sc in next dc, slip st in next slip st, sc in next dc, 2 dc in each of next 2 dc, sc in last dc; join with slip st to first sc, finish off: 36 sts.

BORDER
Rnd 1: With **right** side facing and working in Back Loops Only *(Fig. 28, page 139)*, join Ecru with slip st in marked sc on First Heart; ch 4 (**counts as first tr, now and throughout**), tr in next 3 sc, dc in next 3 sc, hdc in next 2 sc, † sc in next 4 sc, hdc in next dc, ch 1, tr in marked sc on next Heart, dc in next 2 sc, hdc in next 2 sc †, repeat from † to † 19 times **more**, sc in next 3 sc, 3 hdc in next sc, 2 hdc in next dc, sc in next 2 dc, ch 2, skip next 5 sts, sc in next 2 dc, 2 hdc in next dc, 3 hdc in next sc, sc in next 3 sc, hdc in next 2 sc, ★ dc in next 2 sc, tr in next sc, ch 1, skip next 4 sts on **next** Heart, hdc in next sc, sc in next 4 sc, hdc in next 2 sc; repeat from ★ 19 times **more**, dc in next 3 sc, tr in next 4 sc, ch 1, 3 sc around post of last tr made *(Fig. 10, page 135)*, ch 2, 3 sc around post of first tr, ch 1; join with slip to first tr: 444 sts and 44 sps.

Continued on page 24.

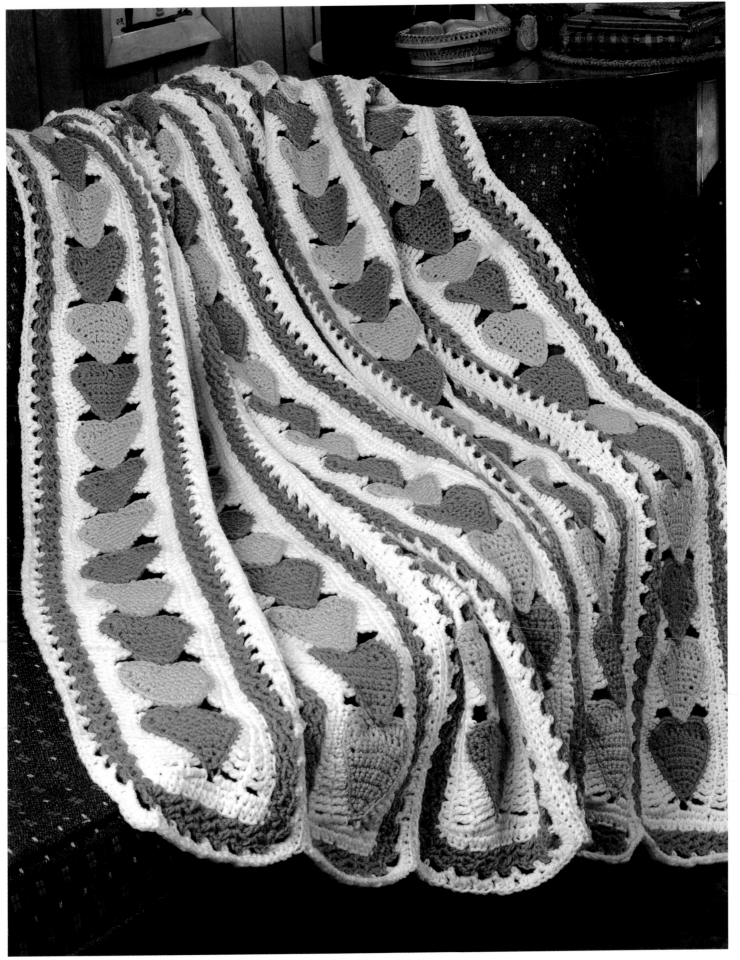

Rnd 2: Ch 4; working in both loops, tr in next 2 tr, dc in next 3 sts, hdc in next 2 sts, (sc in next 6 sts, hdc in next ch-1 sp and in next 4 sts) 20 times, sc in next 5 sts, 3 sc in next corner hdc, sc in next 5 sts, 2 sc in next ch-2 sp, sc in next 5 sts, 3 sc in next corner hdc, sc in next 5 sts, (hdc in next 4 sts and in next ch-1 sp, sc in next 6 sts) 20 times, hdc in next 2 sts, dc in next 3 sts, tr in next 3 tr, ch 1, 3 hdc around post of last tr made, sc in next 3 sc, 2 sc in next ch-2 sp, sc in next 3 sc, 3 hdc around post of first tr, ch 1; join with slip st to first tr: 498 sts and 2 ch-1 sps.

Rnd 3: Ch 2 **(counts as first hdc, now and throughout)**, hdc in each st across to next corner 3-sc group, skip next sc, 3 hdc in center sc, hdc in each st across to center sc of next corner 3-sc group, 3 hdc in center sc, hdc in each st across to last tr, skip last tr, 3 hdc in next ch-1 sp, hdc in next 14 sts, 3 hdc in last ch-1 sp; join with slip st to first hdc, finish off: 506 hdc.

Rnd 4: With **right** side facing, join Blue with slip st in center hdc of corner 3-hdc group at top right of Strip; ch 5 **(counts as first dc plus ch 2)**, sc in same st, (dc, ch 2, sc) in each of next 2 hdc, † [skip next 2 hdc, (dc, ch 2, sc) in next hdc] 4 times, skip next 2 hdc, (dc, ch 2, sc) in each of next 3 hdc, [skip next 2 hdc, (dc, ch 2, sc) in next hdc] 77 times, skip next 2 hdc †, (dc, ch 2, sc) in each of next 3 hdc, repeat from † to † once; join with slip st to first dc: 174 ch-2 sps.

Rnd 5: Slip st in first ch-2 sp, ch 6 **(counts as first dc plus ch 3)**, sc in same sp, (dc, ch 3, sc) in each ch-2 sp around; join with slip st to first dc, finish off: 174 ch-3 sps.

Rnd 6: With **right** side facing, join Ecru with slip st in center ch of first ch-3 sp; ch 1, sc in same ch, ch 4, (sc in center ch of next ch-3 sp, ch 4) around; join with slip st to first sc.

Rnd 7: Slip st in first ch-4 sp, ch 2, 2 hdc in same sp, 7 hdc in next ch-4 sp, 3 hdc in each of next 6 ch-4 sps, 7 hdc in next ch-4 sp, 3 hdc in each of next 79 ch-4 sps, 7 hdc in next ch-4 sp, 3 hdc in each of next 6 ch-4 sps, 7 hdc in next ch-4 sp, 3 hdc in each ch-4 sp across; join with slip st to first hdc, finish off: 538 hdc.

STRIP B (Make 3)
CENTER
Work same as Strip A, reversing colors.

BORDER
Work same as Strip A.

ASSEMBLY
Note: Lay out Strips beginning with Strip A and alternating Strips A and B throughout.

Place two Strips with **wrong** sides together and bottom edges at the same end. Using Ecru and working through inside loops only, whipstitch Strips together *(Fig. 35a, page 141)*, beginning in center hdc of first corner 7-hdc group and ending in center hdc of next corner 7-hdc group.

Join remaining Strips in the same manner, always working in same direction.

VICTORIAN GEM Continued from page 16.

Rnd 6: With **right** side facing, join Dk Rose with slip st in any ch-1 sp; ch 4, dc in same sp, work FPdc around next 10 dc, ★ (dc, ch 1, dc) in next ch-1 sp, work FPdc around next 10 dc; repeat from ★ around; join with slip st to first dc, finish off: 72 dc.

Rnd 7: With **right** side facing, join Ecru with slip st in any ch-1 sp; ch 4, dc in same sp, work BPdc around next 12 dc, ★ (dc, ch 1, dc) in next ch-1 sp, work BPdc around next 12 dc; repeat from ★ around; join with slip st to first dc; do **not** finish off: 84 dc.

Row 8: Ch 1, sc in same st, 2 sc in next ch-1 sp, sc in each dc around working 2 sc in each ch-1 sp; join with slip st to first sc, finish off: 96 sc.

ASSEMBLY

With Ecru and using Placement Diagram as a guide, weave Motifs together *(Figs. 34a & b, page 141)*, forming 6 horizontal strips of 7 Motifs each and 5 horizontal strips of 6 Motifs each, beginning in second sc of first corner and ending in first sc of next corner; weave strips together in same manner.

PLACEMENT DIAGRAM

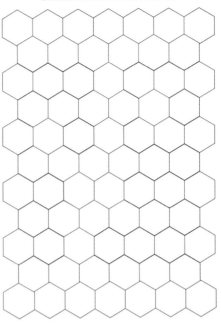

VALENTINE WRAP Continued from page 20.

EDGING

Rnd 1: Ch 1, turn; 2 sc in first sc, ch 1, (skip next sc, sc in next sc, ch 1) across to last 2 sc, skip next sc, 3 sc in last sc; † working in end of rows, ch 1, skip first row, (sc in next row, ch 1, next row) across †; working in free loops of beginning ch *(Fig. 29b, page 139)*, 3 sc in ch at base of first sc, ch 1, ★ skip next ch, sc in next ch, ch 1; repeat from ★ across to last 2 chs, skip next ch, 3 sc in last ch, repeat from † to † once, sc in same st as first sc; join with slip st to first sc: 172 sc.

Rnd 2: Ch 1, turn; 3 sc in same st, ch 1, skip next sc, (sc in next ch-1 sp, ch 1, skip next sc) across to center sc of next corner, ★ 3 sc in center sc, ch 1, (sc in next ch-1 sp, ch 1, skip next sc) across to center sc of next corner; repeat from ★ around; join with slip st to first sc, finish off.

ASSEMBLY

With **right** side of first Panel facing and bottom edge to the right, join yarn with slip st in center sc of first corner 3-sc group; ch 1, holding **second Panel** with **right** side facing and bottom edge to right, slip st in center sc of corresponding corner 3-sc group *(Fig. 32, page 140)*, ch 1, ★ slip st in next ch-1 sp on **first Panel**, ch 1, slip st in next ch-1 sp on **second** Panel, ch 1; repeat from ★ across to next 3-sc group on **both** Panels, skip next sc on **first Panel**, slip st in center sc, ch 1, skip next sc on **second Panel**, slip st in center sc on **second Panel**; finish off.

Join remaining Panel in same manner.

BORDER

Rnd 1: With **right** side facing, join yarn with slip st in center sc of top right corner 3-sc group; ch 1, sc in same st, † ch 1, skip next sc, (sc in next ch-1 sp, ch 1, skip next sc) 12 times, ★ sc in same st as joining on same Strip, ch 1, skip next joining, sc in same st as joining on next Strip, ch 1, skip next sc, (sc in next ch-1 sp, ch 1, skip next sc) 12 times; repeat from ★ once **more**, sc in next sc, ch 1, skip next sc, (sc in next ch-1 sp, ch 1, skip next sc) across to center sc of next corner 3-sc group †, sc in center sc, repeat from † to † once; join with slip st to first sc.

Rnd 2: Ch 1, 3 sc in same st, ch 1, (sc in next ch-1 sp, ch 1) across to next corner sc, ★ 3 sc in corner sc, ch 1, (sc in next ch-1 sp, ch 1) across to next corner sc; repeat from ★ around; join with slip st to first sc.

Rnd 3: Ch 1, sc in same st and in each sc and each ch-1 sp around; join with slip st to first sc, finish off.

FOUR-LEAF CLOVERS

A lucky four-leaf clover created with puff stitches forms the center of each square on this intriguing throw for St. Patrick's Day. The warm wrap is quick to make using a Q hook and holding two strands of brushed acrylic yarn.

STITCH GUIDE

PUFF ST
★ YO, insert hook in sp indicated, YO and pull up a loop even with hook; repeat from ★ 2 times **more**, YO and draw through all 7 loops on hook *(Fig. 19, page 137)*, ch 1 to close .

SQUARE A (Make 32)

Holding two strands of Green together, ch 4; join with slip st to form a ring.

Rnd 1 (Right side): Ch 1, ★ slip st in ring, work Puff St in ring; repeat from ★ 3 times **more**; join with slip st to first slip st, finish off: 4 Puff Sts and 4 slip sts.

Note: Loop a short piece of yarn around any stitch to mark Rnd 1 as **right** side.

Rnd 2: With **right** side facing and holding one strand of Green and one strand of Variegated together, join yarn with slip st in any slip st; ch 2 **(counts as first hdc, now and throughout)**, (hdc, ch 1, 2 hdc) in same st, sc in Back Loop Only of next Puff St *(Fig. 28, page 139)*, ★ (2 hdc, ch 1, 2 hdc) in **both** loops of next slip st, sc in Back Loop Only of next Puff St; repeat from ★ 2 times **more**; join with slip st to first hdc: 20 sts and 4 ch-1 sps.

Rnd 3: Ch 2, (3 hdc, ch 1, 3 hdc) in next ch-1 sp, ★ skip next hdc, hdc in next 3 sts, (3 hdc, ch 1, 3 hdc) in next ch-1 sp; repeat from ★ around to last 3 sts, skip next hdc, hdc in last 2 sts; join with slip st to first hdc, finish off.

SQUARE B (Make 31)

Holding one strand of Green and one strand of Variegated together, ch 4; join with slip st to form a ring.

Rnd 1 (Right side): Ch 1, ★ slip st in ring, work Puff St in ring; repeat from ★ 3 times **more**; join with slip st to first slip st, finish off: 4 Puff Sts and 4 slip sts.

Note: Mark Rnd 1 as **right** side.

Rnd 2: With **right** side facing and holding two strands of Green together, join yarn with slip st in any slip st; ch 2, (hdc, ch 1, 2 hdc) in same st, sc in Back Loop Only of next Puff St, ★ (2 hdc, ch 1, 2 hdc) in **both** loops of next slip st, sc in Back Loop Only of next Puff St; repeat from ★ 2 times **more**; join with slip st to first hdc: 20 sts and 4 ch-1 sps.

Finished Size: 45" x 57"

MATERIALS
Worsted Weight Brushed Acrylic Yarn:
Green - 29$\frac{1}{2}$ ounces,
(840 grams, 2,275 yards)
Variegated - 8 ounces,
(230 grams, 615 yards)
Crochet hook, size Q (15.00 mm)
Yarn needle

GAUGE: Each Square = 6$\frac{1}{4}$"

26

Continued on page 37.

27

MILE-A-MINUTE BLUES

Like prized blue-and-white china, this mile-a-minute throw is destined to become a favorite. A round of white front post treble crochets adds interest to the border of each strip.

Finished Size: 46" x 65"

MATERIALS

Worsted Weight Yarn:

Lt Blue - 26$^{1/2}$ ounces, (750 grams, 1,740 yards)

Blue - 18$^{1/2}$ ounces, (530 grams, 1,215 yards)

White - 9 ounces, (260 grams, 590 yards)

Crochet hooks, sizes G (4.00 mm) **and** I (5.50 mm) **or** sizes needed for gauge

Yarn needle

GAUGE: Center = 1$^{3/4}$" wide and 11 rows = 6"

Each Strip = 3$^{1/4}$" wide

Gauge Swatch: 3$^{1/4}$"w x 8$^{1/2}$"h

Work same as Center for 11 rows.

Finish off.

Work Border.

STITCH GUIDE

> **FRONT POST TREBLE CROCHET (abbreviated FPtr)**
> YO twice, working in **front** of Rnd 1, insert hook from **front** to **back** around post of dc indicated, YO and pull up a loop *(Fig. 13, page 135)*, (YO and draw through 2 loops on hook) 3 times.

STRIP (Make 14)

CENTER

With large size hook and Lt Blue, ch 9 **loosely**.

Row 1: Dc in fourth ch from hook and in next ch **(3 skipped chs count as first dc)**, ch 1, skip next ch, dc in last 3 chs: 6 dc.

Row 2 (Right side): Ch 3 **(counts as first dc, now and throughout)**, turn; dc in next 2 dc, ch 1, dc in last 3 dc.

Note: Loop a short piece of yarn around any stitch to mark Row 2 as **right** side and bottom edge.

Rows 3-115: Ch 3, turn; dc in next 2 dc, ch 1, dc in last 3 dc. Finish off.

BORDER

Rnd 1: With **right** side facing and small size hook, join Blue with sc in ch-1 sp on last row *(see Joining With Sc, page 139)*; (5 dc, sc) in same sp; 5 dc in end of first row, (sc in end of next row, 5 dc in end of next row) across; working over beginning ch, (sc, 5 dc, sc) in next ch-1 sp; 5 dc in end of first row, (sc in end of next row, 5 dc in end of next row) across; join with slip st to Back Loop Only of first sc *(Fig. 28, page 139)*, finish off: 590 dc.

Rnd 2: With **right** side facing, using small size hook, and working in Back Loops Only, join White with sc in second dc to left of joining; 2 sc in next dc, sc in next dc, work FPtr around fifth dc on last row of Center, † skip next 3 sts, sc in next dc, 2 sc in next dc, sc in next dc, working in **front** of Rnd 1, tr around second dc on next row of Center, skip next 3 sts, sc in next dc, 2 sc in next dc, sc in next dc, ★ skip next row on Center, working in **front** of Rnd 1, tr around second dc on next row, skip next 3 sts, sc in next dc, 2 sc in next dc, sc in next dc; repeat from ★ 55 times **more**, work FPtr around second dc on last row of Center, skip next 3 sts †, sc in next dc, 2 sc in next dc, sc in next dc, work FPtr around fifth dc on same row of Center, repeat from † to † once; join with slip st to Back Loop Only of first sc, finish off: 114 tr and 4 FPtr.

Rnd 3: With **right** side facing, using small size hook, and working in Back Loops Only, join Lt Blue with sc in first tr on either side; † place marker around sc just made for joining placement, sc in same st and in each st across to last tr on same side, 2 sc in last tr, place marker around sc just made for joining placement, 2 sc in each of next 14 sts †, sc in next tr, repeat from † to † once; join with slip st to both loops of first sc, finish off.

ASSEMBLY

Place two Strips with **wrong** sides together and bottom edges at the same end. Using Lt Blue and working through inside loops only, whipstitch Strips together *(Fig. 35a, page 141)*, beginning in first marked sc and ending in next marked sc.

Join remaining Strips in same manner, always working in same direction.

EARTH AWAKENS

Like the awakening earth in springtime, this soft throw is light and airy. The lacy mile-a-minute strips are simply whipstitched together and finished with a tailored edging.

Finished Size: 46" x 69"

MATERIALS

Worsted Weight Yarn:
46 ounces, (1,310 grams, 2,685 yards)
Crochet hook, size G (4.00 mm) **or** size needed for gauge
Yarn needle

GAUGE: 16 dc and 8 rows = 4"
Each Strip = 3" wide

STITCH GUIDE

DECREASE
Pull up a loop in next st on same Strip **and** in next st on next Strip, YO and draw through all 3 loops on hook (**counts as one sc**).

STRIP (Make 15)

CENTER

Ch 235 **loosely**.

Row 1 (Right side)**:** Hdc in third ch from hook (**2 skipped chs count as first hdc**) and in each ch across: 234 hdc.
Note: Loop a short piece of yarn around last hdc made to mark bottom edge and to mark Row 1 as **right** side.
Row 2: Ch 4 (**counts as first tr**), turn; ★ YO twice, insert hook in next hdc, YO and pull up a loop, YO and draw through 2 loops on hook, YO, skip next 2 hdc, insert hook in next hdc, YO and pull up a loop (5 loops on hook), (YO and draw through 2 loops on hook) 4 times, ch 2, dc around post of last st made *(Fig. 1)*; repeat from ★ across to last hdc, tr in last hdc: 118 sts and 58 ch-2 sps.
Row 3: Ch 2 (**counts as first hdc**), turn; hdc in next dc and in each ch and each st across; do **not** finish off: 234 hdc.

Fig. 1

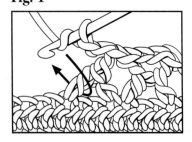

BORDER

Ch 3 (**counts as first dc**), do **not** turn; place marker around dc just made for joining placement, 2 dc in last hdc on Row 3; working in end of rows, skip Row 3, 7 tr in Row 2, skip Row 1; working in free loops of beginning ch *(Fig. 29b, page 139)*, 3 dc in first ch, place marker around last dc made for joining placement, dc in next 233 chs, place marker around last dc made for joining placement, 2 dc in same st; working in end of rows, skip Row 1, 7 tr in Row 2, skip Row 3; working across Row 3, 3 dc in first hdc, place marker around last dc made for joining placement, dc in each hdc across; join with slip st to first dc, finish off: 490 sts.

ASSEMBLY

Place two Strips with **wrong** sides together and bottom edges at the same end. Working through inside loops only, whipstitch Strips together *(Fig. 35a, page 141)*, beginning in first marked dc and ending in next marked dc.

Join remaining Strips in same manner, always working in same direction.

Do **not** remove markers on outside edge of first Strip.

EDGING

With **right** side facing and working in Back Loops Only *(Fig. 28, page 139)*, join yarn with sc in marked dc at top of first Strip *(see Joining With Sc, page 139)*, remove all markers; sc in next 4 sts, † 2 sc in each of next 3 tr, ★ sc in next 3 sts, decrease, sc in next 3 sts, 2 sc in each of next 3 tr; repeat from ★ 13 times **more** †, sc in next 242 sts, repeat from † to † once, sc in each st across; join with slip st to both loops of first sc, finish off.

EASTER EGGS

Wrap up your Easter celebration with this fun springtime throw! The pretty pastel clusters bring to mind colorful Easter eggs hidden on a grassy lawn.

Finished Size: 49" x 71"

MATERIALS
Worsted Weight Yarn:
    White - 9 ounces, (260 grams, 525 yards)
    Green - 28 ounces, (800 grams, 1,635 yards)
    Yellow - 8 ounces, (230 grams, 465 yards)
    Pink - 8 ounces, (230 grams, 465 yards)
    Blue - 9 ounces, (260 grams, 525 yards)
    Purple - 8 ounces, (230 grams, 465 yards)
Crochet hook, size G (4.00 mm) **or** size needed
    for gauge

GAUGE: In pattern, 6 Clusters = 3³/₄" and 8 rows = 4"

Gauge Swatch: 4³/₄"w x 4"h
Ch 17 **loosely**.
Work same as Afghan for 8 rows.

STITCH GUIDE

DECREASE (uses next 2 hdc)
★ YO, insert hook in **next** hdc, YO and pull up a loop, YO and draw through 2 loops on hook; repeat from ★ once **more**, YO and draw through all 3 loops on hook **(counts as one dc)**.

CLUSTER
★ YO, insert hook in sp indicated, YO and pull up a loop, YO and draw through 2 loops on hook; repeat from ★ 2 times **more**, YO and draw through all 4 loops on hook *(Figs. 17a & b, page 136)*.

COLOR SEQUENCE

2 Rows White, 1 row **each**: ★ Green, Yellow, Green, Pink, Green, Blue, Green, Purple, Green, White; repeat from ★ 13 times **more**.

With White, ch 159 **loosely**.

Row 1: Hdc in third ch from hook **(2 skipped chs count as first hdc)**, ★ skip next ch, (hdc, ch 1, hdc) in next ch; repeat from ★ across to last 2 chs, skip next ch, 2 hdc in last ch: 77 ch-1 sps.

Row 2 (Right side): Ch 2 **(counts as first hdc, now and throughout)**, turn; dc in next hdc, ch 1, (work Cluster in next ch-1 sp, ch 1) across to last 3 hdc, skip next hdc, decrease; finish off: 77 Clusters.

Note: Loop a short piece of yarn around any stitch to mark Row 2 as **right** side.

Row 3: With **wrong** side facing, join Green with slip st in first dc; ch 2, (hdc, ch 1, hdc) in next ch-1 sp and in each ch-1 sp across to last 2 sts, skip next dc, hdc in last hdc; finish off: 78 ch-1 sps.

Row 4: With **right** side facing, join next color with slip st in first hdc; ch 4 **(counts as first dc plus ch 1)**, (work Cluster in next ch-1 sp, ch 1) across to last 2 hdc, skip next hdc, dc in last hdc; finish off: 78 Clusters.

Row 5: With **wrong** side facing, join Green with slip st in first dc; ch 2, hdc in next ch-1 sp, (hdc, ch 1, hdc) in next ch-1 sp and in each ch-1 sp across to last ch-1 sp, hdc in last ch-1 sp and in last dc; finish off: 77 ch-1 sps.

Row 6: With **right** side facing, join next color with slip st in first hdc; ch 2, dc in next hdc, ch 1, (work Cluster in next ch-1 sp, ch 1) across to last 3 hdc, skip next hdc, decrease; finish off: 77 Clusters.

Rows 7-142: Repeat Rows 3-6, 34 times.

SWEET RAINBOW

Multicolored rows of clusters form a charming rainbow on this sweet wrap for baby. Puff stitches create a dainty edging for the afghan, which is worked holding two strands of sport weight yarn together.

Finished Size: 36" x 39"

MATERIALS

Sport Weight Yarn:
> White - 17 ounces, (480 grams, 1,605 yards)
> Pink - 2 ounces, (60 grams, 190 yards)
> Peach - 2 ounces, (60 grams, 190 yards)
> Yellow - 2 ounces, (60 grams, 190 yards)
> Green - 2 ounces, (60 grams, 190 yards)
> Blue - 2 ounces, (60 grams, 190 yards)
> Purple - 1¹/₂ ounces, (40 grams, 140 yards)

Crochet hook, size K (6.50 mm) **or** size needed for gauge

GAUGE: In pattern, 6 Clusters and 10 rows = 4"

Gauge Swatch: 4"
Ch 14 **loosely**.
Work same as Afghan for 10 rows.
Finish off.

Note: Entire Afghan is worked holding two strands of yarn together.

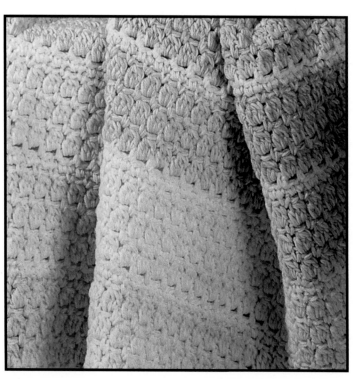

STITCH GUIDE

> **CLUSTER**
> ★ YO, insert hook in sp indicated, YO and pull up a loop, YO and draw through 2 loops on hook; repeat from ★ 2 times **more**, YO and draw through all 4 loops on hook *(Figs. 17a & b, page 136)*.
>
> **PUFF ST**
> ★ YO, insert hook in st indicated, YO and pull up a loop even with loop on hook; repeat from ★ once **more**, YO and draw through all 5 loops on hook *(Fig. 19, page 137)*.

Holding 2 strands of White together, ch 100 **loosely**.

Row 1 (Right side)**:** Sc in second ch from hook and in each ch across: 99 sc.

Note: Loop a short piece of yarn around any stitch to mark Row 1 as **right** side.

Row 2: Ch 1, turn; sc in first sc, ★ ch 1, skip next sc, sc in next sc; repeat from ★ across; finish off: 49 ch-1 sps.

Row 3: Holding one strand of White and one strand of Pink together and with **right** side facing, join yarn with slip st in first sc; ch 3 **(counts as first dc, now and throughout)**, work Cluster in next ch-1 sp, (ch 1, work Cluster in next ch-1 sp) across to last sc, dc in last sc: 49 Clusters and 48 ch-1 sps.

Row 4: Ch 1, turn; sc in first dc, ch 1, (sc in next ch-1 sp, ch 1) across to last dc, sc in last dc: 49 ch-1 sps.

Row 5: Ch 3, turn; work Cluster in next ch-1 sp, (ch 1, work Cluster in next ch-1 sp) across to last sc, dc in last sc.

Rows 6-8: Repeat Rows 4 and 5 once, then repeat Row 4 once **more**.
Finish off.

Row 9: Holding 2 strands of White together and with **right** side facing, join yarn with sc in first sc *(see Joining With Sc, page 139)*; sc in each ch-1 sp and in each sc across: 99 sc.

Row 10: Ch 1, turn; sc in first sc, ★ ch 1, skip next sc, sc in next sc; repeat from ★ across; finish off: 49 ch-1 sps.

Row 11: Holding one strand of White and one strand of Peach together and with **right** side facing, join yarn with slip st in first sc; ch 3, work Cluster in next ch-1 sp, (ch 1, work Cluster in next ch-1 sp) across to last sc, dc in last sc: 49 Clusters and 48 ch-1 sps.

Rows 12-18: Repeat Rows 4-10.

Row 19: Holding one strand of White and one strand of Yellow together and with **right** side facing, join yarn with slip st in first sc; ch 3, work Cluster in next ch-1 sp, (ch 1, work Cluster in next ch-1 sp) across to last sc, dc in last sc: 49 Clusters and 48 ch-1 sps.

Rows 20-26: Repeat Rows 4-10.

Row 27: Holding one strand of White and one strand of Green together and with **right** side facing, join yarn with slip st in first sc; ch 3, work Cluster in next ch-1 sp, (ch 1, work Cluster in next ch-1 sp) across to last sc, dc in last sc: 49 Clusters and 48 ch-1 sps.

Rows 28-34: Repeat Rows 4-10.

Row 35: Holding one strand of White and one strand of Blue together and with **right** side facing, join yarn with slip st in first sc; ch 3, work Cluster in next ch-1 sp, (ch 1, work Cluster in next ch-1 sp) across to last sc, dc in last sc: 49 Clusters and 48 ch-1 sps.

Rows 36-42: Repeat Rows 4-10.

Continued on page 36.

Row 43: Holding one strand of White and one strand of Purple together and with **right** side facing, join yarn with slip st in first sc; ch 3, work Cluster in next ch-1 sp, (ch 1, work Cluster in next ch-1 sp) across to last sc, dc in last sc: 49 Clusters and 48 ch-1 sps.

Rows 44-50: Repeat Rows 4-10.

Rows 51-87: Repeat Rows 3-35 once, then repeat Rows 4-7 once **more**.

Finish off.

Row 88: Holding 2 strands of White together and with **wrong** side facing, join yarn with sc in first dc; ch 1, (sc in next ch-1 sp, ch 1) across to last dc, sc in last dc: 49 ch-1 sps.

Row 89: Ch 1, turn; sc in each sc and in each ch-1 sp across; do **not** finish off: 99 sc.

EDGING

Rnd 1: Ch 1, do **not** turn; work 115 sc evenly spaced across end of rows; working in free loops of beginning ch **(Fig. 29b, page 139)**, 3 sc in first ch, sc in next 97 chs, 3 sc in next ch; work 115 sc evenly spaced across end of rows; working across Row 89, 3 sc in first sc, sc in each sc across to last sc, 3 sc in last sc; join with slip st to Back Loop Only of first sc **(Fig. 28, page 139)**: 436 sc.

Rnd 2: Ch 1, working in Back Loops Only, sc in same st and in each sc across to center sc of next corner, 3 sc in corner sc, ★ sc in each sc across to center sc of next corner, 3 sc in corner sc; repeat from ★ 2 times **more**, sc in last sc; join with slip st to both loops of first sc: 444 sc.

Rnd 3: Pull up loop on hook to measure ½", working in both loops, work Puff St in same st, ch 3, work Puff St in third ch from hook and in same st as first Puff St, skip next 2 sc, ★ (work Puff St in next sc, ch 3, work Puff St in third ch from hook and in same st as first Puff St, skip next 2 sc) across to center sc of next corner, work Puff St in corner sc, (ch 3, work Puff St in third ch from hook and in same st as first Puff St) twice, skip next 2 sc; repeat from ★ around; join with slip st to top of first Puff St, finish off.

FOUR-LEAF CLOVERS Continued from page 26.

Rnd 3: Ch 2, (3 hdc, ch 1, 3 hdc) in next ch-1 sp, ★ skip next hdc, hdc in next 3 sts, (3 hdc, ch 1, 3 hdc) in next ch-1 sp; repeat from ★ around to last 3 sts, skip next hdc, hdc in last 2 sts; join with slip st to first hdc, finish off.

ASSEMBLY

Holding two strands of Green together, using Placement Diagram as a guide, and working through both loops, whipstitch Squares together *(Fig. 35b, page 141)*, forming 7 vertical strips of 9 Squares each, beginning in ch of first corner and ending in ch of next corner; whipstitch strips together in same manner.

PLACEMENT DIAGRAM

A	B	A	B	A	B	A
B	A	B	A	B	A	B
A	B	A	B	A	B	A
B	A	B	A	B	A	B
A	B	A	B	A	B	A
B	A	B	A	B	A	B
A	B	A	B	A	B	A
B	A	B	A	B	A	B
A	B	A	B	A	B	A

EDGING

Rnd 1: With **wrong** side facing, holding two strands of Green together, and working in Front Loops Only, join yarn with slip st in any corner ch; ch 1, ★ 3 sc in corner ch, sc in each sc and each ch across to next corner ch; repeat from ★ around; join with slip st to first sc.

Rnd 2: Turn; working in free loops of each sc and each ch **below** Rnd 1 *(Fig. 29a, page 139)*, 3 sc in first ch, sc in each sc and in each ch across to next corner ch, ★ 3 sc in corner ch, sc in each sc and in each ch across to next corner ch; repeat from ★ around; join with slip st to first sc.

Rnd 3: Do **not** turn; working through **inside** loops of Rnds 1 and 2, slip st in each sc around; join with slip st to first slip st, finish off.

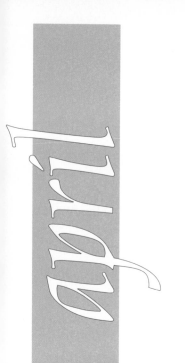

LACY LULLABY

"Somebunny" special will love snuggling up in this precious wrap. Worked in squares with baby sport weight yarn, the afghan has a lacy shell pattern that's created with simple crochet stitches. What a sweet gift for a little one!

Finished Size: 36" x 43"

MATERIALS

Baby Sport Weight Yarn:
   17 ounces, (480 grams, 1,715 yards)
Crochet hook, size G (4.00 mm) **or** size
   needed for gauge
Yarn needle

GAUGE: Each Square = 6¾"

SQUARE (Make 30)

Ch 4; join with slip st to form a ring.

Rnd 1 (Right side)**:** Ch 1, sc in ring, (ch 3, sc in ring) 7 times, ch 1, hdc in first sc to form last ch-3 sp: 8 ch-3 sps.

Note: Loop a short piece of yarn around any stitch to mark Rnd 1 as **right** side.

Rnd 2: Ch 1, 2 sc in same sp, 3 sc in each ch-3 sp around, sc in same sp as first sc; join with slip st to first sc: 24 sc.

Rnd 3: Ch 1, sc in same st, ch 3, skip next 2 sc, ★ (sc, ch 3) twice in next sc, skip next 2 sc; repeat from ★ around, sc in same st as first sc, ch 1, hdc in first sc to form last ch-3 sp: 16 ch-3 sps.

Rnd 4: Ch 3 **(counts as first dc, now and throughout)**, 2 dc in same sp, sc in next ch-3 sp, (5 dc in next ch-3 sp, sc in next ch-3 sp) around, 2 dc in same sp as first dc; join with slip st to first dc: 40 dc and 8 sc.

Rnd 5: Ch 1, sc in same st, ch 3, skip next 2 dc, sc in next sc, ch 3, skip next 2 dc, ★ (sc, ch 3) twice in next dc, skip next 2 dc, sc in next sc, ch 3, skip next 2 dc; repeat from ★ around, sc in same st as first sc, ch 1, hdc in first sc to form last ch-3 sp: 24 ch-3 sps.

Rnd 6: Ch 3, 3 dc in same sp, sc in next ch-3 sp, ch 3, sc in next ch-3 sp, ★ 7 dc in next ch-3 sp, sc in next ch-3 sp, ch 3, sc in next ch-3 sp; repeat from ★ around, 3 dc in same sp as first dc; join with slip st to first dc: 56 dc and 8 ch-3 sps.

Rnd 7: Ch 1, sc in same st, ch 3, (dc, ch 2, dc) in next ch-3 sp, ch 3, skip next 4 sts, sc in next dc, ch 3, (dc, ch 2, dc) in next ch-3 sp, ch 3, skip next 4 sts, ★ (sc, ch 3) twice in next dc, (dc, ch 2, dc) in next ch-3 sp, ch 3, skip next 4 sts, sc in next dc, ch 3, (dc, ch 2, dc) in next ch-3 sp, ch 3, skip next 4 sts; repeat from ★ 2 times **more**, sc in same st as first sc, ch 1, hdc in first sc to form last ch-3 sp: 28 sps.

Rnd 8: Ch 3, 5 dc in same sp, sc in next ch-3 sp, (ch 3, sc in next sp) 5 times, ★ 11 dc in next ch-3 sp, sc in next ch-3 sp, (ch 3, sc in next sp) 5 times; repeat from ★ 2 times **more**, 5 dc in same sp as first dc; join with slip st to first dc: 44 dc and 20 ch-3 sps.

Continued on page 48.

TIMELESS TULIPS

Abloom with the timeless beauty of tulips, this filet crochet throw is simple to cultivate. The flowers are "grown" using a combination of chain spaces and double crochets.

Finished Size: 49" x 74"

MATERIALS
Worsted Weight Yarn:
43 ounces, (1,220 grams, 2,950 yards)
Crochet hook, size I (5.50 mm) **or** size needed for gauge

GAUGE: 17 dc and 9 rows = 4"

Note: Each row is worked across length of Afghan.

BASIC CHART STITCHES
Beginning Block over Block: Ch 3 **(counts as first dc)**, turn; dc in next 3 dc.
Space over Block: Ch 2, skip next 2 dc, dc in next dc.
Block over Block: Dc in next 3 dc.
Space over Space: Ch 2, dc in next dc.
Beginning Increase: Ch 5, turn; dc in fourth ch from hook **(3 skipped chs count as first dc)**, dc in next ch and in next dc.

Block over Space: 2 Dc in next ch-2 sp, dc in next dc.
Ending Increase: ★ YO, insert hook into base of last dc, YO and pull up a loop, YO and draw through one loop on hook, (YO and draw through 2 loops on hook) twice *(Fig. 30, page 139)*; repeat from ★ 2 times **more** (3 dc added).
Beginning and Ending Decrease: Turn; slip st in first 4 dc, ch 3, follow Chart across, leaving last 3 dc unworked.

Ch 291 **loosely**.
Row 1 (Right side)**:** Dc in fourth ch from hook **(3 skipped chs count as first dc)** and in each ch across: 289 dc.
Note: Loop a short piece of yarn around any stitch to mark Row 1 as **right** side.
Rows 2-15: Follow Chart Rows 2-15.
Rows 16-110: Repeat Chart Rows 4-15, 7 times; then repeat Rows 4-14 once **more**.
Row 111: Work Blocks across; finish off.

CHART

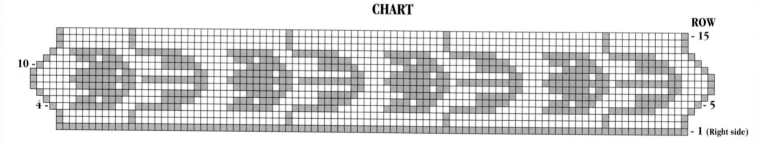

KEY
□ - Space
■ - Block

On right side rows, follow Chart from right to left; on wrong side rows, follow Chart from left to right.

SPRING SPLENDOR

*As green as the new spring grass, this mile-a-minute afghan
works up quickly in strips of worsted weight yarn. The light and
airy spread is splendid for the chilly days of early April.*

Finished Size: 44" x 63"

MATERIALS
Worsted Weight Yarn:
26$\frac{1}{2}$ ounces, (750 grams, 1,815 yards)
Crochet hook, size J (6.00 mm) **or** size needed
for gauge

GAUGE: 16 sc = 5"
Each Strip = 6$\frac{1}{4}$" wide

FIRST STRIP

Ch 182 **loosely.**
Foundation Row (Right side)**:** Sc in back ridge of second ch
from hook and each ch across *(Fig. 2b, page 133)*: 181 sc.
Note: Loop a short piece of yarn around any stitch to mark
Foundation Row as **right** side.
Rnd 1: Ch 1, (sc, ch 3) twice in end of Foundation Row;
working in free loops of beginning ch *(Fig. 29b, page 139)*,
† skip first st, sc in next st, ch 3, skip next st, sc in next st,
★ ch 1, skip next st, sc in next st, ch 3, skip next st, sc in next
st; repeat from ★ 43 times **more** †, ch 3, skip next st, (sc,
ch 3) twice in end of Foundation Row; working across sc on
Foundation Row, repeat from † to † once, ch 1, skip last sc, hdc
in first sc to form last ch-3 sp: 184 sps.
Rnd 2: Slip st in same sp, † ch 1, (dc, ch 1) 6 times in next
ch-3 sp, (slip st in next sp, 5 sc in next ch-3 sp) 45 times †,
slip st in next ch-3 sp, repeat from † to † once; join with slip st
to first slip st: 90 5-sc groups.

Rnd 3: Slip st in first ch-1 sp, ch 2, † (tr in next dc, hdc in next
ch-1 sp) 6 times, ch 1, ★ (hdc, tr, hdc) in center sc of next
5-sc group, ch 1; repeat from ★ 44 times **more** †, hdc in next
ch-1 sp, repeat from † to † once; join with slip st to top of
beginning ch-2: 92 ch-1 sps.
Rnd 4: † (Ch 5, skip next tr, slip st in next hdc) 6 times, ch 1,
dc in next ch-1 sp, (dc, ch 3, dc) in each of next 44 ch-1 sps, dc
in next ch-1 sp, ch 1 †, slip st in next hdc, repeat from † to †
once; join with slip st to base of beginning ch-5: 88 ch-3 sps.
Rnd 5: Slip st in first ch-5 sp, ch 1, 5 sc in same sp and in each
of next 5 ch-5 sps, ch 3, (2 sc, ch 3, 2 sc) in each of next
44 ch-3 sps, ch 3, 5 sc in each of next 6 ch-5 sps, ch 3, (2 sc,
ch 3, 2 sc) in last 44 ch-3 sps, ch 3; join with slip st to first sc,
finish off: 92 ch-3 sps.

REMAINING 6 STRIPS

Work same as First Strip through Rnd 4: 88 ch-3 sps.
Rnd 5 (Joining rnd)**:** Slip st in first ch-5 sp, ch 1, 5 sc in same
sp and in each of next 5 ch-5 sps, ch 3, (2 sc, ch 3, 2 sc) in
each of next 44 ch-3 sps, ch 3, 5 sc in each of next 6 ch-5 sps,
ch 3, ★ 2 sc in next ch-3 sp, ch 1, holding Strips with **wrong**
sides together, slip st in corresponding ch-3 sp on **previous**
Strip *(Fig. 32, page 140)*, ch 1, 2 sc in same sp on **new**
Strip; repeat from ★ across, ch 3; join with slip st to first sc,
finish off.

PRETTY PATTERN

*Basic stitches and an easy pattern make this colorful afghan
a breeze to create! We chose shades of rose for ours, but the worsted
weight wrap can be fashioned in any color to complement your decor.*

Finished Size: 48" x 63"

MATERIALS
Worsted Weight Yarn:
Dk Rose - 11 ounces, (310 grams, 815 yards)
Rose - 14 ounces, (400 grams, 1,040 yards)
Lt Rose - 16 ounces, (450 grams, 1,190 yards)
Crochet hook, size H (5.00 mm) **or** size needed
for gauge

GAUGE: In pattern, 16 sts and 15 rows = 4"

Gauge Swatch: 4"
Ch 17 **loosely**.
Work same as Afghan for 15 rows.

With Dk Rose, ch 193 **loosely**.
Row 1: Sc in second ch from hook, ch 2, ★ skip next 2 chs, sc in next 2 chs, ch 2; repeat from ★ across to last 3 chs, skip next 2 chs, sc in last ch: 96 sc and 48 ch-2 sps.
Row 2 (Right side): Ch 1, turn; sc in first sc, working in **front** of next ch-2, dc in 2 skipped chs one row **below**, ★ ch 2, skip next 2 sc, working in **front** of next ch-2, dc in 2 skipped chs one row **below**; repeat from ★ across to last sc, sc in last sc: 98 sts and 47 ch-2 sps.
Note: Loop a short piece of yarn around any stitch to mark Row 2 as **right** side.
Row 3: Ch 1, turn; sc in first sc, ch 2, ★ skip next 2 dc, working **behind** next ch-2, dc in 2 skipped sc one row **below**, ch 2; repeat from ★ across to last 3 sts, skip next 2 dc, sc in last sc; finish off: 96 sts and 48 ch-2 sps.
Row 4: With **right** side facing, join Rose with sc in first sc *(see Joining With Sc, page 139)*; working in **front** of next ch-2, dc in 2 skipped dc one row **below**, ★ ch 2, skip next 2 dc, working in **front** of next ch-2, dc in 2 skipped dc one row **below**; repeat from ★ across to last sc, sc in last sc: 98 sts and 47 ch-2 sps.
Row 5: Ch 1, turn; sc in first sc, ch 2, ★ skip next 2 dc, working **behind** next ch-2, dc in 2 skipped dc one row **below**, ch 2; repeat from ★ across to last 3 sts, skip next 2 dc, sc in last sc; finish off: 96 sts and 48 ch-2 sps.

Row 6: With **right** side facing, join Lt Rose with sc in first sc; working in **front** of next ch-2, dc in 2 skipped dc one row **below**, ★ ch 2, skip next 2 dc, working in **front** of next ch-2, dc in 2 skipped dc one row **below**; repeat from ★ across to last sc, sc in last sc; finish off: 98 sts and 47 ch-2 sps.
Row 7: With **wrong** side facing, join Rose with sc in first sc; ch 2, ★ skip next 2 dc, working **behind** next ch-2, dc in 2 skipped dc one row **below**, ch 2; repeat from ★ across to last 3 sts, skip next 2 dc, sc in last sc: 96 sts and 48 ch-2 sps.
Row 8: Ch 1, turn; sc in first sc, working in **front** of next ch-2, dc in 2 skipped dc one row **below**, ★ ch 2, skip next 2 dc, working in **front** of next ch-2, dc in 2 skipped dc one row **below**; repeat from ★ across to last sc, sc in last sc; finish off: 98 sts and 47 ch-2 sps.
Row 9: With **wrong** side facing, join Dk Rose with sc in first sc; ch 2, ★ skip next 2 dc, working **behind** next ch-2, dc in 2 skipped dc one row **below**, ch 2; repeat from ★ across to last 3 sts, skip next 2 dc, sc in last sc: 96 sts and 48 ch-2 sps.
Row 10: Ch 1, turn; sc in first sc, working in **front** of next ch-2, dc in 2 skipped dc one row **below**, ★ ch 2, skip next 2 dc, working in **front** of next ch-2, dc in 2 skipped dc one row **below**; repeat from ★ across to last sc, sc in last sc: 98 sts and 47 ch-2 sps.
Row 11: Ch 1, turn; sc in first sc, ch 2, ★ skip next 2 dc, working **behind** next ch-2, dc in 2 skipped dc one row **below**, ch 2; repeat from ★ across to last 3 sts, skip next 2 dc, sc in last sc; finish off: 96 sts and 48 ch-2 sps.
Row 12: With **right** side facing, join Lt Rose with sc in first sc; working in **front** of next ch-2, dc in 2 skipped dc one row **below**, ★ ch 2, skip next 2 dc, working in **front** of next ch-2, dc in 2 skipped dc one row **below**; repeat from ★ across to last sc, sc in last sc; finish off: 98 sts and 47 ch-2 sps.
Rows 13-15: Repeat Rows 9-11.
Row 16: With **right** side facing, join Lt Rose with sc in first sc; working in **front** of next ch-2, dc in 2 skipped dc one row **below**, ★ ch 2, skip next 2 dc, working in **front** of next ch-2, dc in 2 skipped dc one row **below**; repeat from ★ across to last sc, sc in last sc: 98 sts and 47 ch-2 sps.

Continued on page 49.

DANCING DAFFODILS

This breathtaking wrap brings to mind images of dainty daffodils dancing in a meadow. Featuring solid and floral hexagon motifs, the afghan is finished with tassels at the points.

Finished Size: 47" x 71"

MATERIALS

Worsted Weight Yarn:
Green - 38 ounces, (1,080 grams, 2,605 yards)
Yellow - 12 ounces, (340 grams, 825 yards)
Crochet hook, size I (5.50 mm) **or** size needed for gauge
Yarn needle

GAUGE: Each Motif = 4¹/₂"
(straight edge to straight edge)

STITCH GUIDE

DECREASE (uses next 2 sps)
★ YO, insert hook in **next** sp, YO and pull up a loop, YO and draw through 2 loops on hook; repeat from ★ once **more**, YO and draw through all 3 loops on hook (**counts as one dc**).

DAFFODIL MOTIF (Make 60)

Rnd 1 (Right side): With Yellow, ch 2, 6 sc in second ch from hook; do not join, place marker **(see Markers, page 140)**: 6 sc.

Note: Loop a short piece of yarn around any stitch to mark Rnd 1 as **right** side.

Rnd 2: 2 Sc in each sc around: 12 sc.

Rnd 3: Sc in Front Loop Only of each sc around **(Fig. 28, page 139)**.

Rnd 4: Sc in both loops of each sc around.

Rnd 5: (Ch 1, slip st in next sc) around; finish off.

Rnd 6: With **right** side facing and working in free loops on Rnd 2 **(Fig. 29a, page 139)**, join Yellow with sc in any sc **(see Joining With Sc, page 139)**; ch 1, (dc, ch 1, tr) in same st, ch 2, (tr, ch 1, dc, ch 1, sc) in next sc **(Petal made)**, ch 1, ★ (sc, ch 1, dc, ch 1, tr) in next sc, ch 2, (tr, ch 1, dc, ch 1, sc) in next sc, ch 1; repeat from ★ around; join with slip st to first sc, finish off: 6 Petals.

Rnd 7: With **right** side facing, join Green with sc in any ch-1 sp **between** Petals; ch 4, keeping ch-4 **behind** Petals, (sc in ch-1 sp **before** next Petal, ch 4) around; join with slip st to first sc: 6 ch-4 sps.

Rnd 8: Ch 4 (**counts as first dc plus ch 1, now and throughout**), dc in next ch-4 sp, ch 1, sc in ch-2 sp on first Petal, ch 1, dc in same ch-4 sp, ch 1, ★ dc in next sc, ch 1, dc in next ch-4 sp, ch 1, sc in ch-2 sp on next Petal, ch 1, dc in same ch-4 sp, ch 1; repeat from ★ around; join with slip st to first dc: 24 ch-1 sps.

Rnd 9: Slip st in first ch-1 sp, ch 4, dc in next ch-1 sp, ch 3, ★ dc in next ch-1 sp, (ch 1, dc in next ch-1 sp) 3 times, ch 3; repeat from ★ 4 times **more**, (dc in next ch-1 sp, ch 1) twice; join with slip st to first dc, finish off: 18 ch-1 sps and 6 ch-3 sps.

SOLID MOTIF (Make 102)

Rnd 1 (Right side): With Green, ch 2, 6 sc in second ch from hook; join with slip st to first sc: 6 sc.

Note: Mark Rnd 1 as **right** side.

Rnd 2: Ch 4, dc in same st, ch 1, (dc, ch 1) twice in each sc around; join with slip st to first dc: 12 ch-1 sps.

Rnd 3: Slip st in first ch-1 sp, ch 6 (**counts as first dc plus ch 3, now and throughout**), dc in same sp, ch 1, dc in next ch-1 sp, ch 1, ★ (dc, ch 3, dc) in next ch-1 sp, ch 1, dc in next ch-1 sp, ch 1; repeat from ★ around; join with slip st to first dc: 12 ch-1 sps and 6 ch-3 sps.

Rnd 4: Slip st in first ch-3 sp, ch 6, dc in same sp, ch 1, (dc in next ch-1 sp, ch 1) twice, ★ (dc, ch 3, dc) in next ch-3 sp, ch 1, (dc in next ch-1 sp, ch 1) twice; repeat from ★ around; join with slip st to first dc, finish off: 18 ch-1 sps and 6 ch-3 sps.

HALF MOTIF (Make 16)

Row 1 (Right side): With Green, ch 6, (dc, ch 1) 4 times in sixth ch from hook (**5 skipped chs count as first tr plus ch 1**), tr in same ch: 5 ch-1 sps.

Note: Mark Row 1 as **right** side.

Row 2: Ch 5 (**counts as first tr plus ch 1, now and throughout**), turn; dc in next ch-1 sp, ch 1, ★ (dc, ch 3, dc) in next ch-1 sp, ch 1, dc in next ch-1 sp, ch 1; repeat from ★ once **more**, tr in last tr: 6 ch-1 sps and 2 ch-3 sps.

Row 3: Ch 5, turn; (dc in next ch-1 sp, ch 1) twice, ★ (dc, ch 3, dc) in next ch-3 sp, ch 1, (dc in next ch-1 sp, ch 1) twice; repeat from ★ once **more**, tr in last tr: 9 ch-1 sps and 2 ch-3 sps.

Continued on page 48.

DANCING DAFFODILS Continued from page 46.

Edging: Ch 3, do **not** turn; working across end of rows, sc around post of tr just made (corner made), ch 1, (sc in top of next tr, ch 1) twice, sc around post of same tr, ch 1, sc around post of next tr, ch 1, sc in top of same tr, ch 1, sc in top of next tr, ch 1, sc around post of next tr, ch 3; join with slip st to top of same tr (corner made), finish off: 7 ch-1 sps and 2 ch-3 sps.

PLACEMENT DIAGRAM

A

KEY
⬡ - **Solid Motif**
⬡ - **Daffodil Motif**
▭ - **Half Motif**

ASSEMBLY
With Green, working through both loops, and using Placement Diagram as a guide, whipstitch Motifs together, forming 17 horizontal strips *(Fig. 35b, page 141)*, beginning in center ch of first corner and ending in center ch of next corner; whipstitch strips together in same manner.

EDGING
Rnd 1: With **right** side facing, join Green with slip st in first ch-1 sp on long edge (Point A on Placement Diagram); ch 4, ★ (dc in next sp, ch 1) across to next corner ch-3 sp, (dc, ch 3, dc) in corner ch-3 sp, ch 1, (dc in next ch-1 sp, ch 1) 3 times, (dc, ch 3, dc) in next ch-3 sp, ch 1, (dc in next ch-1 sp, ch 1) 3 times, † decrease, ch 1, (dc in next ch-1 sp, ch 1) 3 times, (dc, ch 3, dc) in next ch-3 sp, ch 1, (dc in next ch-1 sp, ch 1) 3 times †, repeat from † to † across to next corner ch-3 sp, (dc, ch 3, dc) in corner ch-3 sp, ch 1; repeat from ★ once **more**; join with slip st to first dc.
Rnd 2: Slip st in first ch-1 sp, ch 1, sc in same sp, ch 1, ★ (sc in next ch-1 sp, ch 1) across to next ch-3 sp, (sc, ch 1) twice in ch-3 sp; repeat from ★ around to last ch-1 sp, sc in ch-1 sp, ch 1; join with slip st to first sc, finish off.

Holding 12 strands of Green together, add fringe in each point across short edges of Afghan *(Figs. 36a & c, page 142)*.

LACY LULLABY Continued from page 38.

Rnd 9: Ch 1, sc in same st, ch 3, skip next 2 dc, sc in next dc, ch 3, (sc in next ch-3 sp, ch 3) 5 times, skip next 3 sts, sc in next dc, ch 3, skip next 2 dc, ★ (sc, ch 3) twice in next dc, skip next 2 dc, sc in next dc, ch 3, (sc in next ch-3 sp, ch 3) 5 times, skip next 3 sts, sc in next dc, ch 3, skip next 2 dc; repeat from ★ 2 times **more**, sc in same st as first sc, ch 1, hdc in first sc to form last ch-3 sp: 36 ch-3 sps.
Rnd 10: Ch 3, 2 dc in same sp, ★ † 3 dc in each of next 2 ch-3 sps, 3 hdc in each of next 4 ch-3 sps, 3 dc in each of next 2 ch-3 sps †, (3 dc, ch 3, 3 dc) in next ch-3 sp; repeat from ★ 2 times **more**, then repeat from † to † once, 3 dc in same sp as first dc, ch 3; join with slip st to first dc, finish off: 120 sts and 4 ch-3 sps.

ASSEMBLY
Working through both loops, whipstitch Squares together, forming 5 vertical strips of 6 Squares each *(Fig. 35b, page 141)*, beginning in center ch of first corner ch-3 and ending in center ch of next corner ch-3; whipstitch strips together in same manner.

EDGING

Rnd 1: With **right** side facing, join yarn with sc in any corner ch-3 sp *(see Joining With Sc, page 139)*; ch 3, ★ † skip next 3 sts, [sc in sp **before** next st *(Fig. 33, page 140)*, ch 3, skip next 3 sts] 9 times, [sc in next joining, ch 3, skip next 3 sts, (sc in sp **before** next st, ch 3, skip next 3 sts) 9 times] across to next corner ch-3 sp †, (sc, ch 3) twice in corner ch-3 sp; repeat from ★ 2 times **more**, then repeat from † to † once, sc in same sp as first sc, ch 1, hdc in first sc to form last ch-3 sp: 224 ch-3 sps.

Rnds 2-4: Ch 1, sc in same sp, ch 3, (sc in next ch-3 sp, ch 3) across to next corner ch-3 sp, ★ (sc, ch 3) twice in corner ch-3 sp, (sc in next ch-3 sp, ch 3) across to next corner ch-3 sp; repeat from ★ 2 times **more**, sc in same sp as first sc, ch 1, hdc in first sc to form last ch-3 sp: 236 ch-3 sps.

Rnd 5: Ch 3, 3 dc in same sp, sc in next ch-3 sp, (5 dc in next ch-3 sp, sc in next ch-3 sp) across to next corner ch-3 sp, ★ 7 dc in corner ch-3 sp, sc in next ch-3 sp, (5 dc in next ch-3 sp, sc in next ch-3 sp) across to next corner ch-3 sp; repeat from ★ 2 times **more**, 3 dc in same sp as first dc; join with slip st to first dc, finish off.

PRETTY PATTERN Continued from page 44.

Row 17: Ch 1, turn; sc in first sc, ch 2, ★ skip next 2 dc, working **behind** next ch-2, dc in 2 skipped dc one row **below**, ch 2; repeat from ★ across to last 3 sts, skip next 2 dc, sc in last sc: 96 sts and 48 ch-2 sps.

Row 18: Ch 1, turn; sc in first sc, working in **front** of next ch-2, dc in 2 skipped dc one row **below**, ★ ch 2, skip next 2 dc, working in **front** of next ch-2, dc in 2 skipped dc one row **below**; repeat from ★ across to last sc, sc in last sc; finish off: 98 sts and 47 ch-2 sps.

Row 19: With **wrong** side facing, join Rose with sc in first sc; ch 2, ★ skip next 2 dc, working **behind** next ch-2, dc in 2 skipped dc one row **below**, ch 2; repeat from ★ across to last 3 sts, skip next 2 dc, sc in last sc: 96 sts and 48 ch-2 sps.

Row 20: Ch 1, turn; sc in first sc, working in **front** of next ch-2, dc in 2 skipped dc one row **below**, ★ ch 2, skip next 2 dc, working in **front** of next ch-2, dc in 2 skipped dc one row **below**; repeat from ★ across to last sc, sc in last sc; finish off: 98 sts and 47 ch-2 sps.

Row 21: With **wrong** side facing, join Lt Rose with sc in first sc; ch 2, ★ skip next 2 dc, working **behind** next ch-2, dc in 2 skipped dc one row **below**, ch 2; repeat from ★ across to last 3 sts, skip next 2 dc, sc in last sc; finish off: 96 sts and 48 ch-2 sps.

Row 22: With **right** side facing, join Rose with sc in first sc; working in **front** of next ch-2, dc in 2 skipped dc one row **below**, ★ ch 2, skip next 2 dc, working in **front** of next ch-2, dc in 2 skipped dc one row **below**; repeat from ★ across to last sc, sc in last sc; finish off: 98 sts and 47 ch-2 sps.

Row 23: With **wrong** side facing, join Lt Rose with sc in first sc; ch 2, ★ skip next 2 dc, working **behind** next ch-2, dc in 2 skipped dc one row **below**, ch 2; repeat from ★ across to last 3 sts, skip next 2 dc, sc in last sc; finish off: 96 sts and 48 ch-2 sps.

Row 24: With **right** side facing, join Rose with sc in first sc; working in **front** of next ch-2, dc in 2 skipped dc one row **below**, ★ ch 2, skip next 2 dc, working in **front** of next ch-2, dc in 2 skipped dc one row **below**; repeat from ★ across to last sc, sc in last sc: 98 sts and 47 ch-2 sps.

Row 25: Ch 1, turn; sc in first sc, ch 2, ★ skip next 2 dc, working **behind** next ch-2, dc in 2 skipped dc one row **below**, ch 2; repeat from ★ across to last 3 sts, skip next 2 dc, sc in last sc; finish off: 96 sts and 48 ch-2 sps.

Rows 26-28: Repeat Rows 16-18.

Rows 29-35: Repeat Rows 9-15.

Rows 36-233: Repeat Rows 4-35, 6 times; then repeat Rows 4-9 once **more**.

Row 234: Ch 1, turn; sc in first sc, working in **front** of next ch-2, dc in 2 skipped dc one row **below**, ★ sc in next 2 dc, working in **front** of next ch-2, dc in 2 skipped dc one row **below**; repeat from ★ across to last sc, sc in last sc; finish off.

EDGING

Top: With **right** side facing, join Dk Rose with slip st in first sc on last row; ch 1, ★ skip next st, slip st in next st, ch 1; repeat from ★ across to last 3 sts, skip next dc, slip st in last 2 sts; finish off.

Bottom: With **right** side facing and working in free loops of beginning ch *(Fig. 29b, page 139)*, join Dk Rose with slip st in ch at base of first sc; ch 1, ★ skip next ch, slip st in next ch, ch 1, repeat from ★ across to last 3 chs, skip next ch, slip st in last 2 chs; finish off.

LIGHT AND LACY

Light and lacy, this mile-a-minute afghan makes a delicate addition to the bedroom. The quick-to-make throw, crocheted in strips using basic stitches, looks absolutely dreamy in soft white.

Finished Size: 47" x 66"

MATERIALS
Worsted Weight Yarn:
  38 ounces,
    (1,080 grams, 2,605 yards)
Crochet hook, size J (6.00 mm) **or** size needed for gauge

GAUGE: 12 sc = 4"
  Each Strip = 4¹/₄" wide

FIRST STRIP

Ch 190 **loosely**.

Foundation Row (Right side): Sc in back ridge of second ch from hook and each ch across *(Fig. 2b, page 133)*: 189 sc.

Note: Loop a short piece of yarn around any stitch to mark Foundation Row as **right** side.

Rnd 1: (Slip st, ch 3, 2 dc) in end of Foundation Row; working in free loops of beginning ch *(Fig. 29b, page 139)*, † (slip st, ch 3, 2 dc) in first st, ★ skip next 2 sts,(slip st, ch 3, 2 dc) in next st; repeat from ★ 61 times **more**, skip next 2 sts †, (slip st, ch 3, 2 dc) in end of Foundation Row; working across sc on Foundation Row, repeat from † to † once; join with slip st to first slip st: 128 ch-3 sps.

Rnd 2: Slip st in first 3 chs, ch 1, (sc in same sp, ch 3) twice, (sc in next ch-3 sp, ch 3) 63 times, (sc, ch 3) twice in next ch-3 sp, (sc in next ch-3 sp, ch 3) across; join with slip st to first sc: 130 ch-3 sps.

Rnd 3: Ch 1, sc in same st, (dc, ch 3, dc) in next ch-3 sp, ★ sc in next sc, (dc, ch 3, dc) in next ch-3 sp; repeat from ★ around; join with slip st to first sc.

Rnd 4: Slip st in next dc, ★ [slip st, ch 3, slip st, ch 2, 3 dc, ch 2, (slip st, ch 3) twice] in next ch-3 sp, (slip st, ch 3) 3 times in next ch-3 sp, (slip st, ch 3) twice in each of next 62 ch-3 sps, (slip st, ch 3) 3 times in next ch-3 sp; repeat from ★ once **more**; join with slip st to first slip st, finish off: 266 ch-3 sps.

REMAINING 10 STRIPS

Work same as First Strip through Rnd 3: 130 ch-3 sps.

Rnd 4 (Joining rnd)**:** Slip st in next dc, † [slip st, ch 3, slip st, ch 2, 3 dc, ch 2, (slip st, ch 3) twice] in next ch-3 sp, (slip st, ch 3) 3 times in next ch-3 sp †, (slip st, ch 3) twice in each of next 62 ch-3 sps, (slip st, ch 3) 3 times in next ch-3 sp, repeat from † to † once, slip st in next ch-3 sp, ch 1, holding Strips with **wrong** sides together, slip st in corresponding ch-3 sp on **previous Strip** *(Fig. 32, page 140)*, ch 1, slip st in same sp on **new Strip**, ch 3, ★ slip st in next ch-3 sp, ch 1, skip next ch-3 sp on **previous Strip**, slip st in next ch-3 sp, ch 1, slip st in same sp on **new Strip**, ch 3; repeat from ★ across to last ch-3 sp, (slip st, ch 3) 3 times in last ch-3 sp; join with slip st to first slip st, finish off.

OLD-TIME CHARM

Brimming with old-fashioned charm, this heirloom afghan is worked in squares using soft brushed acrylic yarn. Front post treble crochets create the ornamental floral motifs in the centers of the squares.

Finished Size: 50" x 71"

MATERIALS

Worsted Weight Brushed Acrylic Yarn:
  Rose - 39 ounces, (1,110 grams, 1,755 yards)
  Cream - 33 ounces, (940 grams, 1,485 yards)
Crochet hook, size H (5.00 mm) **or** size needed
  for gauge
Yarn needle

GAUGE SWATCH: Each Square = 7"

STITCH GUIDE

> **FRONT POST TREBLE CROCHET**
> **(abbreviated FPtr)**
> YO twice, insert hook from **front** to **back** around post of st indicated, YO and pull up a loop **(Fig. 13, page 135)**, (YO and draw through 2 loops on hook) 3 times.

SQUARE (Make 70)

Rnd 1 (Right side)**:** With Rose, ch 4, 11 dc in fourth ch from hook; join with slip st to top of beginning ch: 12 sts.

Note: Loop a short piece of yarn around any stitch to mark Rnd 1 as **right** side.

Rnd 2: Ch 3 **(counts as first dc, now and throughout)**, dc in same st, 2 dc in each dc around; join with slip st to first dc, finish off: 24 dc.

Rnd 3: With **right** side facing, join Cream with slip st in same st as joining; ch 3, work FPtr around first st on Rnd 1, ★ skip st behind FPtr, dc in next dc, work FPtr around next dc on Rnd 1; repeat from ★ around to last dc, skip last dc; join with slip st to first dc: 12 FPtr.

Rnd 4: Ch 3, dc in same st, work FPtr around next FPtr, ★ 2 dc in next dc, work FPtr around next FPtr; repeat from ★ around; join with slip st to first dc, finish off: 24 dc.

Rnd 5: With **right** side facing and working in Back Loops Only **(Fig. 28, page 139)**, join Rose with slip st in first dc of any 2-dc group; ch 3, 2 dc in next dc, work FPtr around next FPtr, ★ dc in next dc, 2 dc in next dc, work FPtr around next FPtr; repeat from ★ around; join with slip st to first dc, finish off: 36 dc.

Rnd 6: With **right** side facing and working in both loops, join Cream with slip st in any FPtr; ch 3, 3 dc in same st, 4 dc in next FPtr, (4 tr, ch 2, 4 tr) in next FPtr, ★ 4 dc in each of next 2 FPtr, (4 tr, ch 2, 4 tr) in next FPtr; repeat from ★ around; join with slip st to first dc, finish off: 64 sts and 4 ch-2 sps.

Rnd 7: With **right** side facing, join Rose with slip st in any corner ch-2 sp; ch 3, (2 dc, ch 2, 3 dc) in same sp, working in Back Loops Only, dc in next 4 tr, [dc in sp **before** next st **(Fig. 33, page 140)**, dc in next 4 sts] 3 times, ★ (3 dc, ch 2, 3 dc) in next ch-2 sp, dc in next 4 tr, (dc in sp **before** next st, dc in next 4 sts) 3 times; repeat from ★ around; join with slip st to first dc, finish off: 100 dc.

ASSEMBLY

Using Rose and working through inside loops only, whipstitch Squares together, forming 7 vertical strips of 10 Squares each **(Fig. 35a, page 141)**, beginning in second ch of first corner ch-2 and ending in first ch of next corner ch-2; whipstitch strips together in same manner.

EDGING

Rnd 1: With **right** side facing, join Cream with sc in any corner ch-2 sp **(see Joining with Sc, page 139)**; 2 sc in same sp, working in Back Loops Only, sc in next 25 dc, (sc in next sp, ch 2, sc in next sp and in next 25 dc) across to next corner ch-2 sp, ★ 3 sc in corner ch-2 sp, sc in next 25 dc, (sc in next sp, ch 2, sc in next sp and in next 25 dc) across to next corner ch-2 sp; repeat from ★ around; join with slip st to first sc, finish off: 922 sc.

Rnd 2: With **right** side facing and working in Back Loops Only, join Rose with sc in any sc; sc in each sc and in each ch around working 3 sc in center sc of each corner 3-sc group; join with slip st to both loops of first sc, finish off.

LILAC GARDEN

The magnificence of garden lilacs inspired this lacy throw.
V-Stitches and popcorns mirror the beauty of the fragrant flowers,
and popcorns and shells create the intricate floral edging.

Finished Size: 46" x 60"

MATERIALS
Worsted Weight Yarn:
    61 ounces, (1,730 grams, 4,185 yards)
Crochet hook, size G (4.00 mm) **or** size needed
    for gauge
Yarn needle

GAUGE: One repeat (3 Popcorns and 3 V-Sts)
    and 8 rows = 3"

Gauge Swatch: 6¹/₂"w x 4¹/₄"h
Ch 41 **loosely**.
Work same as Center for 11 rows.

STITCH GUIDE

> **V-ST**
> (Dc, ch 1, dc) in st or sp indicated.
> **POPCORN**
> 5 Dc in sp indicated, drop loop from hook, insert hook in first dc of 5-dc group, hook dropped loop and draw through **(Fig. 18b, page 136)**. When Popcorn is worked on **wrong** side row, push Popcorn to **right** side.
> **BEGINNING SHELL**
> Slip st in next dc and in next ch-2 sp, ch 3, (dc, ch 2, 2 dc) in same sp.
> **SHELL**
> (2 Dc, ch 2, 2 dc) in sp indicated.

CENTER

Ch 221 **loosely**.
Row 1 (Right side)**:** Dc in fourth ch from hook **(3 skipped chs count as first dc)**, (skip next 2 chs, work V-St in next ch) across to last 4 chs, skip next 2 chs, dc in last 2 chs: 71 V-Sts and 4 dc.
Note: Loop a short piece of yarn around any stitch to mark Row 1 as **right** side.
Row 2: Ch 3 **(counts as first dc, now and throughout)**, turn; dc in same st, work V-St in next ch-1 sp, ch 5, skip next ch-1 sp, sc in next ch-1 sp, ch 5, ★ skip next ch-1 sp, work V-St in each of next 3 ch-1 sps, ch 5, skip next ch-1 sp, sc in next ch-1 sp, ch 5; repeat from ★ 10 times **more**, skip next ch-1 sp, work V-St in next ch-1 sp, skip next 2 dc, 2 dc in last dc: 35 ch-1 sps and 24 ch-5 sps.
Row 3: Ch 3, turn; dc in same st, work V-St in next ch-1 sp, ch 3, (sc in next ch-5 sp, ch 3) twice, ★ work V-St in each of next 3 ch-1 sps, ch 3, (sc in next ch-5 sp, ch 3) twice; repeat from ★ 10 times **more**, work V-St in next ch-1 sp, skip next 2 dc, 2 dc in last dc: 35 ch-1 sps and 36 ch-3 sps.
Row 4: Ch 3, turn; dc in same st, work V-St in next ch-1 sp, skip next ch-3 sp, work Popcorn in next ch-3 sp, (ch 2, work Popcorn in same sp) twice, ★ skip next ch-3 sp, work V-St in each of next 3 ch-1 sps, skip next ch-3 sp, work Popcorn in next ch-3 sp, (ch 2, work Popcorn in same sp) twice; repeat from ★ 10 times **more**, skip next ch-3 sp, work V-St in next ch-1 sp, skip next 2 dc, 2 dc in last dc: 36 Popcorns.
Row 5: Ch 3, turn; dc in same st, work V-St in next ch-1 sp, ch 3, (sc in next ch-2 sp, ch 3) twice, ★ work V-St in each of next 3 ch-1 sps, ch 3, (sc in next ch-2 sp, ch 3) twice; repeat from ★ 10 times **more**, work V-St in next ch-1 sp, skip next 2 dc, 2 dc in last dc: 35 ch-1 sps and 36 ch-3 sps.
Row 6: Ch 3, turn; dc in same st, work V-St in next ch-1 sp, work V-St in center ch of each of next 3 ch-3, ★ work V-St in each of next 3 ch-1 sps, work V-St in center ch of each of next 3 ch-3; repeat from ★ 10 times **more**, work V-St in next ch-1 sp, skip next 2 dc, 2 dc in last dc: 71 V-Sts and 4 dc.
Rows 7-136: Repeat Rows 2-6, 26 times.
Do **not** finish off.

EDGING

Rnd 1: Ch 1, turn; 4 sc in first dc, work 212 sc evenly spaced across to last dc, 4 sc in last dc; work 302 sc evenly spaced across end of rows; working in free loops of beginning ch **(Fig. 29b, page 139)**, 4 sc in first ch, work 212 sc evenly spaced across to ch at base of first dc, 4 sc in ch at base of first dc; work 302 sc evenly spaced across end of rows; join with slip st to first sc: 1,044 sc.
Rnd 2: Ch 3, do **not** turn; dc in next sc, ch 2, dc in next 2 sc, ch 5, skip next 5 sc, ★ dc in next 2 sc, ch 2, dc in next 2 sc, ch 5, skip next 5 sc; repeat from ★ around; join with slip st to first dc: 116 ch-2 sps and 116 ch-5 sps.

Continued on page 59.

ELEGANCE FOR MOTHER

Remember Mother on her special day with this exquisite Victorian-style wrap. The timeless treasure features a closely woven pattern of shells and an elegant edging of fanciful fans. Regal tassels accent the corners of the afghan.

Finished Size: 47" x 60"

MATERIALS

Worsted Weight Yarn:
 51 ounces, (1,450 grams, 2,975 yards)
Crochet hook, size G (4.00 mm) **or** size needed
 for gauge
Yarn needle

GAUGE: For Center, in pattern, 21 sts (2 repeats)
 and 12 rows = 4"
 For Edging, 16 sc = 4"

Gauge Swatch: 4"
Ch 22 **loosely**.
Work same as Center for 12 rows.
Finish off.

STITCH GUIDE

SHELL
(3 Dc, ch 1, 3 dc) in st indicated.
V-ST
(Hdc, ch 1, hdc) in next ch-1 sp.
PICOT
Ch 4, slip st in fourth ch from hook.

CENTER

Ch 182 **loosely**.
Row 1 (Right side): Sc in second ch from hook and in next ch, skip next 3 chs, work Shell in next ch, ★ skip next 3 chs, sc in next ch, ch 1, skip next ch, sc in next ch, skip next 3 chs, work Shell in next ch; repeat from ★ across to last 5 chs, skip next 3 chs, sc in last 2 chs: 18 Shells.
Note: Loop a short piece of yarn around any stitch to mark Row 1 as **right** side.
Row 2: Ch 2 **(counts as first hdc, now and throughout)**, turn; hdc in same st, ch 3, sc in next Shell (ch-1 sp), ch 3, ★ work V-St, ch 3, sc in next Shell, ch 3; repeat from ★ across to last 2 sc, skip next sc, 2 hdc in last sc: 17 V-Sts.
Row 3: Ch 3 **(counts as first dc, now and throughout)**, turn; 3 dc in same st, sc in next ch-3 sp, ch 1, sc in next ch-3 sp, ★ work Shell in next V-St (ch 1-sp), sc in next ch-3 sp, ch 1, sc in next ch-3 sp; repeat from ★ across to last 2 hdc, skip next hdc, 4 dc in last hdc: 17 Shells.

56

Row 4: Ch 1, turn; sc in first dc, ch 3, work V-St, ch 3, ★ sc in next Shell, ch 3, work V-St, ch 3; repeat from ★ across to last 4 dc, skip next 3 dc, sc in last dc: 18 V-Sts.
Row 5: Ch 1, turn; sc in first sc and in next ch-3 sp, work Shell in next V-St, ★ sc in next ch-3 sp, ch 1, sc in next ch-3 sp, work Shell in next V-St; repeat from ★ across to last ch-3 sp, sc in last ch-3 sp and in last sc: 18 Shells.
Repeat Rows 2-5 until Center measures 46¹/₂" from beginning ch, ending by working Row 5; do **not** finish off.

EDGING

Rnd 1: Ch 1, do **not** turn; work 183 sc evenly spaced across end of rows; 3 sc in free loop of first ch *(Fig. 29b, page 139)*, working over beginning ch, work 129 sc evenly spaced across to next corner ch, 3 sc in free loop of corner ch; work 183 sc evenly spaced across end of rows; working in sts across last row, 3 sc in first sc, work 129 sc evenly spaced across to last sc, 3 sc in last sc; join with slip st to first sc: 636 sc.
Rnd 2: Ch 5, skip next 2 sc, working in Back Loops Only *(Fig. 28, page 139)*, (dc in next sc, ch 2, skip next 2 sc) around; join with slip st to third ch of beginning ch-5, finish off: 212 ch-2 sps.

FANS
FIRST FAN

Ch 6; join with slip st to form a ring.
Row 1: Ch 3, 13 dc in ring; do **not** join: 14 dc.
Row 2 (Right side): Ch 3, turn; dc in same st, 2 dc in next dc and in each dc across: 28 dc.
Note: Mark Row 2 as **right** side.
Row 3: Ch 3, turn; dc in next 2 dc, (ch 5, skip next 2 dc, dc in next 3 dc) across: 5 ch-5 sps.
Row 4: Ch 5 **(counts as first dc plus ch 2, now and throughout)**, turn; work Shell in center ch of next ch-5, (ch 7, work Shell in center ch of next ch-5) across to last 3 dc, ch 2, skip next 2 dc, dc in last dc: 5 Shells.
Row 5: Ch 5, turn; work Shell in next Shell, (ch 8, work Shell in next Shell) across to last 4 dc, ch 2, skip next 3 dc and next ch-2 sp, dc in last dc.

Continued on page 58.

ELEGANCE FOR MOTHER Continued from page 56.

Row 6: Ch 5, turn; work Shell in next Shell, (ch 10, work Shell in next Shell) across to last 4 dc, ch 2, skip next 3 dc and next ch-2 sp, dc in last dc.

Row 7: Ch 1, turn; sc in first dc, ch 5, sc in next Shell, ★ ch 8, sc around ch-sps of last 3 rows, ch 8, sc in next Shell; repeat from ★ across to last 4 dc, ch 5, skip next 3 dc and next ch-2 sp, sc in last dc.

Row 8: Ch 1, turn; sc in first sc, ch 5, (dc, work Picot, dc) in next sc, ch 5, ★ work Shell in next sc, ch 5, (dc, work Picot, dc) in next sc, ch 5; repeat from ★ across to last sc, sc in last sc.

Row 9: Ch 5, turn; (dc, work Picot) 3 times in next Picot (ch-4 sp), ★ ch 7, work Shell in next Shell, ch 7, (dc, work Picot) 3 times in next Picot; repeat from ★ across to last sc, ch 2, dc in last sc.

Row 10: Ch 5, turn; sc in next Picot, ch 3, (sc, ch 6, sc) in next Picot, ch 3, sc in next Picot, ★ ch 9, work Shell in next Shell, ch 9, sc in next Picot, ch 3, (sc, ch 6, sc) in next Picot, ch 3, sc in next Picot; repeat from ★ across to last 2 dc, ch 2, skip next dc, dc in last dc.

Row 11: Ch 5, turn; skip next ch-2 sp, sc in next ch-3 sp, ch 3, (sc, ch 6, sc) in next ch-6 sp, ch 3, sc in next ch-3 sp, ★ ch 11, work Shell in next Shell, ch 11, sc in next ch-3 sp, ch 3, (sc, ch 6, sc) in next ch-6 sp, ch 3, sc in next ch-3 sp; repeat from ★ across to last sc, skip last sc, ch 2, dc in last dc.

Row 12: Ch 1, turn; sc in first dc, ch 3, skip next ch-2 sp, sc in next ch-3 sp, ch 3, (sc, ch 6, sc) in next ch-6 sp, place marker around ch-6 just made for Fan joining, ch 3, sc in next ch-3 sp, ch 7, sc around ch-sps of last 4 rows, ch 7, (sc in next dc, ch 3) 3 times, sc in next ch-1 sp, (ch 3, sc in next dc) 3 times, ★ ch 7, sc around ch-sps of last 4 rows, ch 7, sc in next ch-3 sp, ch 3, (sc, ch 6, sc) in next ch-6 sp, ch 3, sc in next ch-3 sp, ch 7, sc around ch-sps of last 4 rows, ch 7, (sc in next dc, ch 3) 3 times, sc in next ch-1 sp, (ch 3, sc in next dc) 3 times; repeat from ★ 2 times **more**, place marker around last ch-3 made for Corner placement, ch 7, sc around ch-sps of last 4 rows, ch 7, sc in next ch-3 sp, ch 3, (sc, ch 6, sc) in next ch-6 sp, place marker around ch-6 just made for Last Fan joining, ch 3, sc in next ch-3 sp, ch 3, sc in last dc; finish off.

NEXT 12 FANS

Work same as First Fan through Rnd 11.

Row 12 (Joining rnd): Ch 1, turn; sc in first dc, ch 3, skip next ch-2 sp, sc in next ch-3 sp, ch 3, (sc, ch 6, sc) in next ch-6 sp, place marker around ch-6 just made for Fan joining, ch 3, sc in next ch-3 sp, ch 7, sc around ch-sps of last 4 rows, ch 7, (sc in next dc, ch 3) 3 times, sc in next ch-1 sp, (ch 3, sc in next dc) 3 times, ★ ch 7, sc around ch-sps of last 4 rows, ch 7, sc in next ch-3 sp, ch 3, (sc, ch 6, sc) in next ch-6 sp, ch 3, sc in next ch-3 sp, ch 7, sc around ch-sps of last 4 rows, ch 7, (sc in next dc, ch 3) 3 times, sc in next ch-1 sp, (ch 3, sc in next dc) 3 times; repeat from ★ 2 times **more**, place marker around last ch-3 made for Corner placement, ch 7, sc around ch-sps of last 4 rows, ch 7, sc in next ch-3 sp, ch 3, sc in next ch-6 sp, ch 3, holding **previous Fan** with **right** side facing, slip st in marked ch-6 sp of **previous Fan**, remove marker, ch 3, sc in same sp of **new Fan**, ch 3, sc in next ch-3 sp, ch 3, sc in last dc, ch 4, slip st in first sc of **previous Fan**; finish off.

LAST FAN

Work same as First Fan through Rnd 11.

Row 12 (Joining rnd): Ch 1, turn; sc in first dc, ch 4, holding First Fan with **right** side facing, slip st in last sc of **First Fan**, slip st in 4 chs just made and in first sc of **Last Fan**, ch 3, skip next ch-2 sp, sc in next ch-3 sp, ch 3, sc in next ch-6 sp, ch 3, slip st in marked ch-6 sp of **First Fan**, remove marker, ch 3, sc in same sp of **Last Fan**, ch 3, sc in next ch-3 sp, ch 7, sc around ch-sps of last 4 rows, ch 7, (sc in next dc, ch 3) 3 times, sc in next ch-1 sp, (ch 3, sc in next dc) 3 times, ★ ch 7, sc around ch-sps of last 4 rows, ch 7, sc in next ch-3 sp, ch 3, (sc, ch 6, sc) in next ch-6 sp, ch 3, sc in next ch-3 sp, ch 7, sc around ch-sps of last 4 rows, ch 7, (sc in next dc, ch 3) 3 times, sc in next ch-1 sp, (ch 3, sc in next dc) 3 times; repeat from ★ 2 times **more**, place marker around last ch-3 made for Corner Placement, ch 7, sc around ch-sps of last 4 rows, ch 7, sc in next ch-3 sp, ch 3, sc in next ch-6 sp, ch 3, holding **previous Fan** with **right** side facing and being careful not to twist Fans, slip st in marked ch-6 sp of **previous Fan**, remove marker, ch 3, sc in same sp of **Last Fan**, ch 3, sc in next ch-3 sp, ch 3, sc in last dc, ch 4, slip st in first sc of **previous Fan**; finish off.

CORNER

Row 1: With **right** side facing, join yarn with slip st in any marked ch-3 sp; ch 3, skip next ch-7 sp, sc in next ch-7 sp, ch 3, (sc in next ch-sp, ch 3) 4 times, sc in next ch-7 sp, ch 3, skip next ch-7 sp, slip st in next ch-3 sp, leave remaining sts unworked: 7 ch-3 sps.

Rows 2-5: Turn; slip st in first ch-3 sp, ch 1, sc in same sp, (ch 3, sc in next ch-3 sp) across: 3 ch-3 sps.

Row 6: Turn; slip st in first ch-3 sp, ch 1, sc in same sp, (ch 3, sc in next ch-3 sp) twice: 2 ch-3 sps.

Row 7: Turn; slip st in first ch-3 sp, ch 1, sc in same sp, ch 7, in fourth ch from hook work (slip st, ch 5, slip st, ch 3, slip st), ch 3, sc in last ch-3 sp; finish off.

Using Placement Diagram as a guide, repeat for remaining 3 Corners.

Remove remaining markers.

PLACEMENT DIAGRAM

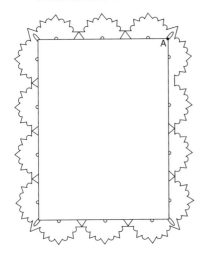

EDGING

With **right** side facing and working along inside edge of Fans, join yarn with slip st at Point A; ch 1, 3 sc in same sp, † work 183 sc evenly spaced across to next corner, work 3 sc in corner sp; work 129 sc evenly spaced across to next corner †, 3 sc in corner sp, repeat from † to † once; join with slip st to first sc, finish off: 636 sc.

FINISHING

With **wrong** sides together and working through inside loops only, whipstitch Center Edging and Fan Edging together, being careful to match corners *(Fig. 35a, page 141)*.

Attach Tassel to each corner *(Figs. 37a & b, page 142)*.

LILAC GARDEN Continued from page 54.

Rnd 3: Work beginning Shell, ch 5, skip next ch-5 sp, dc in next ch-2 sp, (ch 1, dc in same sp) 5 times, ch 5, skip next ch-5 sp, ★ work Shell in next ch-2 sp, ch 5, skip next ch-5 sp, dc in next ch-2 sp, (ch 1, dc in same sp) 5 times, ch 5, skip next ch-5 sp; repeat from ★ around; join with slip st to first dc: 58 Shells and 290 ch-1 sps.

Rnd 4: Work beginning Shell, ch 5, skip next ch-5 sp, work Popcorn in next ch-1 sp, (ch 2, work Popcorn in next ch-1 sp) 4 times, ch 5, skip next ch-5 sp, ★ work Shell in next ch-2 sp, ch 5, skip next ch-5 sp, work Popcorn in next ch-1 sp, (ch 2, work Popcorn in next ch-1 sp) 4 times, ch 5, skip next ch-5 sp; repeat from ★ around; join with slip st to first dc: 290 ch-2 sps and 116 ch-5 sps.

Rnd 5: Work beginning Shell, ch 2, 2 dc in same sp, ch 5, skip next ch-5 sp, work Popcorn in next ch-2 sp, (ch 2, work Popcorn in next ch-2 sp) 3 times, ch 5, skip next ch-5 sp, ★ 2 dc in next ch-2 sp, (ch 2, 2 dc in same sp) twice, ch 5, skip next ch-5 sp, work Popcorn in next ch-2 sp, (ch 2, work Popcorn in next ch-2 sp) 3 times, ch 5, skip next ch-5 sp; repeat from ★ around; join with slip st to first dc: 232 Popcorns.

Rnd 6: Work beginning Shell, ch 3, work Shell in next ch-2 sp, ch 5, skip next ch-5 sp, work Popcorn in next ch-2 sp, (ch 2, work Popcorn in next ch-2 sp) twice, ch 5, skip next ch-5 sp, ★ work Shell in next ch-2 sp, ch 3, work Shell in next ch-2 sp, ch 5, skip next ch-5 sp, work Popcorn in next ch-2 sp, (ch 2, work Popcorn in next ch-2 sp) twice, ch 5, skip next ch-5 sp; repeat from ★ around; join with slip st to first dc: 174 Popcorns and 116 Shells.

Rnd 7: Work beginning Shell, ch 5, sc in next ch-3 sp, ch 5, work Shell in next ch-2 sp, ch 5, skip next ch-5 sp, work Popcorn in next ch-2 sp, ch 2, work Popcorn in next ch-2 sp, ch 5, skip next ch-5 sp, ★ work Shell in next ch-2 sp, ch 5, sc in next ch-3 sp, ch 5, work Shell in next ch-2 sp, ch 5, skip next ch-5 sp, work Popcorn in next ch-2 sp, ch 2, work Popcorn in next ch-2 sp, ch 5, skip next ch-5 sp; repeat from ★ around; join with slip st to first dc: 174 ch-2 sps and 232 ch-5 sps.

Rnd 8: Work beginning Shell, ch 5, (sc in next ch-5 sp, ch 5) twice, work Shell in next ch-2 sp, ch 5, skip next ch-5 sp, work Popcorn in next ch-2 sp, ch 5, skip next ch-5 sp, ★ work Shell in next ch-2 sp, ch 5, (sc in next ch-5 sp, ch 5) twice, work Shell in next ch-2 sp, ch 5, skip next ch-5 sp, work Popcorn in next ch-2 sp, ch 5, skip next ch-5 sp; repeat from ★ around; join with slip st to first dc: 116 ch-2 sps and 290 ch-5 sps.

Rnd 9: Work beginning Shell, ch 5, (sc in next ch-5 sp, ch 5) 3 times, work Shell in next ch-2 sp, ch 5, skip next ch-5 sp, sc in next Popcorn, ch 5, skip next ch-5 sp, ★ work Shell in next ch-2 sp, ch 5, (sc in next ch-5 sp, ch 5) 3 times, work Shell in next ch-2 sp, ch 5, skip next ch-5 sp, sc in next Popcorn, ch 5, skip next ch-5 sp; repeat from ★ around; join with slip st to first dc: 116 ch-2 sps and 348 ch-5 sps.

Rnd 10: Work beginning Shell, ch 5, (sc in next ch-5 sp, ch 5) 4 times, work Shell in next ch-2 sp, ch 1, skip next 2 ch-5 sps, ★ work Shell in next ch-2 sp, ch 5, (sc in next ch-5 sp, ch 5) 4 times, work Shell in next ch-2 sp, ch 1, skip next 2 ch-5 sps; repeat from ★ around; join with slip st to first dc: 290 ch-5 sps.

Rnd 11: Slip st in next dc and in next ch-2 sp, ch 1, sc in same sp and in next ch-5 sp, (7 dc in next ch-5 sp, sc in next ch-5 sp) twice, sc in next ch-2 sp, work Shell in next ch-1 sp, ★ sc in next ch-2 sp and in next ch-5 sp, (7 dc in next ch-5 sp, sc in next ch-5 sp) twice, sc in next ch-2 sp, work Shell in next ch-1 sp; repeat from ★ around; join with slip st to first sc, finish off.

DREAMY SHELLS

Fashioned with soft brushed acrylic yarn, this summery throw will have you dreaming of romance. The easy-to-crochet strips are bordered with showy shells.

STITCH GUIDE

SHELL
5 Dc in st or sp indicated.

STRIP (Make 11)

CENTER
Ch 8 **loosely**.

Row 1: Dc in fourth ch from hook **(3 skipped chs count as first dc)** and in each ch across: 6 dc.

Row 2 (Right side): Ch 3 **(counts as first dc, now and throughout)**, turn; dc in Back Loop Only of next dc and each dc across *(Fig. 28, page 139)*.

Note: Loop a short piece of yarn around any stitch to mark Row 2 as **right** side and bottom edge.

Row 3: Ch 3, turn; dc in Front Loop Only of next dc and each dc across.

Row 4: Ch 3, turn; dc in Back Loop Only of next dc and each dc across.

Rows 5-105: Repeat Rows 3 and 4, 50 times; then repeat Row 3 once **more**.

Do **not** finish off.

BORDER

Rnd 1: Ch 3, turn; 4 dc in same st, skip next 2 dc, sc in sp **before** next dc *(Fig. 33, page 140)*, skip next 2 dc, work Shell in last dc; working in end of rows, sc in first row, (work Shell in next row, sc in next row) across; working in free loops of beginning ch *(Fig. 29b, page 139)*, work Shell in ch at base of first dc, skip next 2 chs, sc in sp **before** next dc, skip next 2 chs, work Shell in last ch; working in end of rows, sc in first row, (work Shell in next row, sc in next row) across; join with slip st to first dc: 108 Shells.

Rnd 2: Slip st in next 2 dc, ch 1, sc in same st, ch 5, sc in next sc, ch 5, sc in center dc of next Shell, (ch 3, sc in center dc of next Shell) 53 times, ch 5, sc in next sc, ch 5, (sc in center dc of next Shell, ch 3) across; join with slip st to first sc: 110 sc and 110 sps.

Continued on page 71.

Finished Size: 45" x 60"

MATERIALS
Worsted Weight Brushed Acrylic Yarn:
     35 ounces, (990 grams, 2,700 yards)
Crochet hook, size G (4.00 mm) **or** size needed for gauge

GAUGE: 16 dc and 8 rows = 4"
          Each Strip = 4" wide

UNITED IN LOVE

With its interlocking rings symbolizing the sacred union of marriage, this delicate throw is the perfect wedding gift for a special couple. What a thoughtful reminder of their precious promises!

Finished Size: 45" x 60"

MATERIALS
Sport Weight Yarn:
  White - 16 ounces, (450 grams, 1,510 yards)
  Ecru - 13 ounces, (370 grams, 1,225 yards)
Crochet hook, size H (5.00 mm) **or** size needed for gauge

GAUGE: Each Motif (through Rnd 1 of Edging) = 4¼" x 5¼"

STITCH GUIDE

PICOT
Ch 3, sc in third ch from hook.

FIRST MOTIF
FIRST RING
With Ecru, ch 18; join with slip st to form a ring.
Rnd 1 (Right side): Ch 2 **(counts as first hdc, now and throughout)**, 31 hdc in ring; join with slip st to first hdc: 32 hdc.
Note: Loop a short piece of yarn around any stitch to mark Rnd 1 as **right** side.
Rnd 2: Slip st in next hdc and in each hdc around; join with slip st to first slip st.
Rnd 3: Ch 1, working **behind** slip sts and in hdc on Rnd 1, sc in same st, place marker around sc just made for Edging placement, † work Picot, skip next hdc, sc in next hdc †, repeat from † to † 5 times **more**, place marker around last sc made for Edging placement, repeat from † to † 9 times, work Picot, skip last hdc; join with slip st to first sc, finish off: 16 sc.

SECOND RING
With Ecru, ch 18; with **right** side of First Ring facing, insert end of ch from **front** to **back** through center of First Ring; join with slip st to form a ring.
Rnds 1-3: Work same as First Ring: 16 sc.

EDGING
Rnd 1: With **right** side of **both** Rings facing you, holding Rings together matching **first** marked sc on Second Ring with **second** marked sc on First Ring, and working through **both** Rings, join White with slip st in marked sc, remove markers; ch 6 **(counts as first dc plus ch 3, now and throughout)**, sc in third ch from hook **(counts as first Picot, now and throughout)**; working through one Ring only, (dc in next sc, work Picot) 9 times; working through **both** Rings, dc in next marked sc, remove markers, work Picot; working through one Ring only, (dc in next sc, work Picot) 9 times; join with slip st to first dc: 20 dc.
Note: Two different colors of markers are recommended, using the same color for each type of joining specified.
Rnd 2: Ch 6, sc in third ch from hook, dc in same st, ch 1, (dc, work Picot, dc) in next dc, place marker around last Picot made for bottom joining, ch 1, [(dc, work Picot, dc) in next dc, ch 1] 5 times, place marker around last Picot made for side joining, [(dc, work Picot, dc) in next dc, ch 1] around; join with slip st to first dc, finish off: 20 Picots.

ADDITIONAL MOTIFS
Work same as First Motif through Rnd 1 of Edging: 20 dc.
Note: Two different colors of markers are recommended, using the same color for each type of joining specified.
Rnd 2: Work Bottom, One Side, or Two Side Joining, arranging Motifs as follows: 7 vertical rows of 11 Motifs each.

BOTTOM JOINING
Rnd 2 (Joining rnd): Ch 6, sc in third ch from hook, dc in same st, ch 1, (dc, work Picot, dc) in next dc, place marker around last Picot made for bottom joining, ch 1, [(dc, work Picot, dc) in next dc, ch 1] 5 times, place marker around last Picot made for side joining, [(dc, work Picot, dc) in next dc, ch 1] twice, dc in next dc, ch 1, holding Motifs with **wrong** sides together, sc in Picot marked for bottom joining on **adjacent Motif** *(Fig. 32, page 140)*, remove marker, ch 1, sc in last ch on **new Motif**, dc in same st as last dc, ch 1, ★ dc in next dc, ch 1, sc in next Picot on **adjacent Motif**, ch 1, sc in last ch on **new Motif**, dc in same st as last dc, ch 1; repeat from ★ once **more**, [(dc, work Picot, dc) in next dc, ch 1] around; join with slip st to first dc, finish off.

Continued on page 71.

DAD'S COMFY WRAP

*Why not surprise Dad with this handsome afghan on
Father's Day! He'll love curling up for a nap with the wrap, which
is crocheted in squares and then assembled in strips. We chose
comfy brushed acrylic yarn in tan and cream for a masculine look.*

Finished Size: 55" x 68"

MATERIALS
Worsted Weight Brushed Acrylic Yarn:
  Cream - 35 ounces, (990 grams, 1,575 yards)
  Tan - 33 ounces, (940 grams, 1,485 yards)
Crochet hook, size H (5.00 mm) **or** size needed
  for gauge
Yarn needle

GAUGE: Each Square = 7"

Gauge Swatch: 4¹/₄"
Work same as Square Rnds 1-4.

STITCH GUIDE

> **FRONT POST TREBLE CROCHET**
> *(abbreviated FPtr)*
> YO twice, insert hook from **front** to **back** around post of st
> indicated, YO and pull up a loop *(Fig. 13, page 135)*, (YO
> and draw through 2 loops on hook) 3 times. Skip st behind
> FPtr.
>
> **FRONT POST DOUBLE CROCHET**
> *(abbreviated FPdc)*
> YO, insert hook from **front** to **back** around post of st
> indicated, YO and pull up a loop *(Fig. 12, page 135)*, (YO
> and draw through 2 loops on hook) twice. Skip st behind
> FPdc.

SQUARE (Make 45)
Rnd 1 (Right side)**:** With Cream, ch 4, 11 dc in fourth ch from
hook; join with slip st to top of beginning ch: 12 sts.
Note: Loop a short piece of yarn around any stitch to mark
Rnd 1 as **right** side.
Rnd 2: Ch 3 **(counts as first dc, now and throughout)**,
2 dc in same st, 3 dc in next dc, ch 3, skip next dc, (3 dc in
each of next 2 dc, ch 3, skip next dc) around; join with slip st to
first dc, finish off: 24 dc.

Rnd 3: With **right** side facing, join Tan with slip st in any
ch-3 sp; ch 3, 4 dc in same sp, skip next dc, dc in next dc, work
FPtr around dc on Rnd 1 **below** dc just made and around next
dc, dc in next dc on Rnd 2, skip next dc, ★ 5 dc in next ch-3 sp,
skip next dc, dc in next dc, work FPtr around dc on Rnd 1
below dc just made and around next dc, dc in next dc on
Rnd 2, skip next dc; repeat from ★ around; join with slip st to
first dc, finish off: 28 dc and 8 FPtr.
Rnd 4: With **right** side facing, join Cream with slip st in center
dc of any 5-dc group; ch 3, (2 dc, ch 3, 3 dc) in same st, ch 1,
skip next 2 dc, dc in next dc, work FPdc around each of next
2 FPtr, dc in next dc, ch 1, skip next 2 dc, ★ (3 dc, ch 3, 3 dc)
in next dc, ch 1, skip next 2 dc, dc in next dc, work FPdc
around each of next 2 FPtr, dc in next dc, ch 1, skip next 2 dc;
repeat from ★ around; join with slip st to first dc, finish off:
32 dc and 8 FPdc.
Rnd 5: With **right** side facing, join Tan with slip st in any
corner ch-3 sp; ch 4 **(counts as first tr, now and
throughout)**, (3 dc, ch 3, 3 dc, tr) in same sp, ch 1, skip next
3 dc and next ch-1 sp, dc in next dc, work FPdc around each of
next 2 FPdc, dc in next dc, ch 1, ★ (tr, 3 dc, ch 3, 3 dc, tr) in
next ch-3 sp, ch 1, skip next 3 dc and next ch-1 sp, dc in next
dc, work FPdc around each of next 2 FPdc, dc in next dc, ch 1;
repeat from ★ around; join with slip st to first tr, finish off:
48 sts and 12 sps.
Rnd 6: With **right** side facing, join Cream with slip st in any
corner ch-3 sp; ch 4, (4 dc, ch 3, 4 dc, tr) in same sp, ch 1,
skip next 4 sts and next ch-1 sp, 2 dc in next dc, work FPdc
around each of next 2 FPdc, 2 dc in next dc, ch 1, ★ (tr, 4 dc,
ch 3, 4 dc, tr) in next ch-3 sp, ch 1, skip next 4 sts and next
ch-1 sp, 2 dc in next dc, work FPdc around each of next 2 FPdc,
2 dc in next dc, ch 1; repeat from ★ around; join with slip st to
first tr, finish off: 64 sts and 12 sps.
Rnd 7: With **right** side facing, join Tan with sc in any corner
ch-3 sp *(see Joining With Sc, page 139)*; 4 sc in same sp,
working in Back Loops Only *(Fig. 28, page 139)*, sc in each st
and in each ch around working 5 sc in each corner ch-3 sp;
join with slip st to first sc, finish off: 92 sc.

Continued on page 72.

ROCK-A-BYE ROSES

This charming afghan is a sweet present for baby. Accented with dimensional roses, the sport weight throw has an openwork pattern created with simple shells and picots. It's finished with a lacy ruffled edging.

Finished Size: 36" x 46"

MATERIALS
Sport Weight Yarn:
    White - 19 ounces, (540 grams, 1,790 yards)
    Pink - 3/4 ounce, (20 grams, 70 yards)
    Green - 1/2 ounce, (15 grams, 45 yards)
Crochet hook, size F (3.75 mm) **or** size needed
    for gauge
Yarn needle

GAUGE: In pattern, (Shell, sc) 3 times
         and 14 rows = 4¼"

Gauge Swatch: 4¾"w x 4¼"h
Ch 31 **loosely.**
Work same as Afghan for 14 rows.
Finish off.

STITCH GUIDE

PICOT
Ch 3, sc in third ch from hook.
SHELL
(3 Dc, ch 2, 3 dc) in ch-6 sp indicated.
BACK POST SINGLE CROCHET (abbreviated BPsc)
Insert hook from **back** to **front** around post of sc indicated **(Fig. 10, page 135)**, YO and pull up a loop, YO and draw through both loops on hook.

With White, ch 175 **loosely.**

Row 1 (Right side)**:** Dc in fourth ch from hook (**3 skipped chs count as first dc**), ★ ch 3, skip next 3 chs, (sc, work Picot, sc) in next ch, ch 3, skip next 3 chs, dc in next 2 chs; repeat from ★ across: 40 dc, 38 ch-3 sps, and 19 Picots.

Row 2: Ch 1, turn; sc in first dc, ch 1, sc in next ch-3 sp, ch 6, sc in next ch-3 sp, ch 1, ★ sc in next ch-3 sp, ch 6, sc in next ch-3 sp, ch 1; repeat from ★ across to last 2 dc, skip next dc, sc in last dc: 19 ch-6 sps and 20 ch-1 sps.

Row 3: Ch 1, turn; sc in first sc and in next ch-1 sp, work Shell in next ch-6 sp, ★ sc in next ch-1 sp, work Shell in next ch-6 sp; repeat from ★ across to last ch-1 sp, sc in last ch-1 sp and last sc: 19 Shells.

Row 4: Ch 3 (**counts as first dc, now and throughout**), turn; dc in same st, ch 3, (sc, work Picot, sc) in next ch-2 sp, ch 3, ★ 2 dc in next sc, ch 3, (sc, work Picot, sc) in next ch-2 sp, ch 3; repeat from ★ across to last 5 sts, skip next 4 sts, 2 dc in last sc: 40 dc, 38 ch-3 sps, and 19 Picots.

Rows 5-120: Repeat Rows 2-4, 38 times; then repeat Rows 2 and 3 once **more.**

Row 121: Ch 3, turn; dc in same st, ch 3, sc in next ch-2 sp, ch 3, ★ 2 dc in next sc, ch 3, sc in next ch-2 sp, ch 3; repeat from ★ across to last 5 sts, skip next 4 sts, 2 dc in last sc; do **not** finish off: 40 dc and 19 sc.

EDGING

Rnd 1: Ch 1, do **not** turn; † working in end of rows, (sc, ch 5, sc) in first row (corner made), ch 3, (skip next row, sc in next row, ch 3) across to last 2 rows, skip next row, (sc, ch 5, sc) in last row, ch 3 †; working in free loops of beginning ch **(Fig. 29b, page 139)**, skip first 5 chs, sc in next ch, ch 3, ★ skip next 3 chs, sc in next ch, ch 3, skip next 4 chs, sc in next ch, ch 3; repeat from ★ across to last 5 chs, skip last 5 chs, repeat from † to † once; working across sts on Row 121, sc in next sc, ch 3, (sc in next dc, ch 3, sc in next sc, ch 3) across; join with slip st to first sc: 196 ch-3 sps and 4 ch-5 sps.

Rnd 2: Slip st in first sp, ch 1, (sc in same sp, ch 6) 6 times, † [sc in next ch-3 sp, ch 6, (sc, ch 6) twice in next ch-3 sp] across to next corner ch-5 sp, (sc, ch 6) 6 times in corner ch-5 sp, (sc in next ch-3 sp, ch 6) twice †, [(sc, ch 6) twice in next ch-3 sp, sc in next ch-3 sp, ch 6] across to next corner ch-5 sp, (sc, ch 6) 6 times in corner ch-5 sp, repeat from † to † once, (sc, ch 6) twice in next ch-3 sp, sc in next ch-3 sp, [ch 6, (sc, ch 6) twice in next ch-3 sp, sc in next ch-3 sp] across, ch 3, dc in first sc to form last ch-6 sp: 316 ch-6 sps.

Rnds 3-5: Ch 1, sc in same sp, (ch 6, sc in next ch-6 sp) around, ch 3, dc in first sc to form last ch-6 sp.

Rnd 6: Ch 1, (sc, work Picot, sc) in same sp, ★ ch 6, (sc, work Picot, sc) in next ch-6 sp; repeat from ★ around, ch 3, dc in first sc to form last ch-6 sp.

Continued on page 73.

ROSY TRELLIS

June is National Rose Month, and our pretty pastel afghan celebrates this beloved flower. The intricate pattern resembles a trellis covered with the summer blooms.

Finished Size: 47" x 63"

MATERIALS

Worsted Weight Yarn:
Pink - 17 ounces, (480 grams, 990 yards)
Blue - 15 ounces, (430 grams, 875 yards)
Green - 17 ounces, (480 grams, 990 yards)
Off-White - 19 ounces, (540 grams, 1,110 yards)
Crochet hook, size H (5.00 mm) **or** size needed for gauge
Yarn needle

GAUGE: 3 repeats on Rnd 1 = 5¼"
Each Strip = 5¼" wide

STITCH GUIDE

BEGINNING SPLIT TREBLE CROCHET
(abbreviated beginning Split tr)
YO twice, insert hook from **back** to **front** in marked ch, YO and pull up a loop, (YO and draw through 2 loops on hook) twice, YO twice, insert hook from **front** to **back** in next ch indicated, YO and pull up a loop, (YO and draw through 2 loops on hook) twice, YO and draw through all 3 loops on hook *(Figs. 22a & b, page 137)*.

SPLIT TREBLE CROCHET
(abbreviated Split tr)
YO twice, working in **front** of last 3 dc made, insert hook from **back** to **front** in same ch as last Split tr made, YO and pull up a loop, (YO and draw through 2 loops on hook) twice, YO twice, insert hook from **front** to **back** in next ch indicated, YO and pull up a loop, (YO and draw through 2 loops on hook) twice, YO and draw through all 3 loops on hook *(Figs. 23a & b, page 137)*.

ENDING SPLIT TREBLE CROCHET
(abbreviated ending Split tr)
YO twice, working in **front** of last 3 dc made, insert hook from **back** to **front** in same ch as last Split tr made, YO and pull up a loop, (YO and draw through 2 loops on hook) twice, YO twice, insert hook from **front** to **back** in first marked ch,

YO and pull up a loop, (YO and draw through 2 loops on hook) twice, YO and draw through all 3 loops on hook *(Figs. 24a & b, page 138)*.

SPLIT TREBLE CROCHET CLUSTER
(abbreviated Split tr Cluster)
YO twice, working in **front** of last 3 dc made, insert hook from **back** to **front** in center of previous Split tr, YO and pull up a loop, (YO and draw through 2 loops on hook) twice, YO twice, skip next 3 dc, insert hook from **front** to **back** in center of next Split tr, YO and pull up a loop, (YO and draw through 2 loops on hook) twice, YO and draw through all 3 loops on hook *(Figs. 25a & b, page 138)*.

FRONT POST TREBLE CROCHET
(abbreviated FPtr)
YO twice, insert hook from **front** to **back** around post of st indicated, YO and pull up a loop *(Fig. 13, page 135)*, (YO and draw through 2 loops on hook) 3 times.

FRONT POST HALF DOUBLE CROCHET
(abbreviated FPhdc)
YO, insert hook from **front** to **back** around post of st indicated, YO and pull up a loop *(Fig. 11, page 135)*, YO and draw through all 3 loops on hook. Skip st behind FPhdc.

Continued on page 70.

STRIP (Make 9)

Foundation Row (Right side): With Pink, ch 5, place marker in first ch made for st placement, tr in fourth ch from hook **(3 skipped chs count as one tr, now and throughout)**, ★ ch 5, tr in fourth ch from hook; repeat from ★ 31 times **more**: 33 2-tr groups.

Note: Loop a short piece of yarn around last stitch made to mark top edge and to mark Foundation Row as **right** side. Do **not** remove markers unless otherwise instructed.

Rnd 1: Ch 4, 2 dc in fourth ch from hook, place marker in ch just worked into for st placement; working around each tr and in each unworked ch between 2-tr groups, 3 dc around first tr, work beginning Split tr, working **behind** beginning Split tr just made, 3 dc around same tr, † 3 dc around next tr, work Split tr, working **behind** Split tr just made, 3 dc around same tr †, repeat from † to † across to last tr, 3 dc around last tr, work ending Split tr, 3 dc around same tr, 3 dc in marked ch; working around each tr and in free loops of each ch between 2-tr groups (at base of Split tr on opposite side) *(Fig. 29b, page 139)*, 3 dc around first tr, work beginning Split tr, remove marker, working **behind** beginning Split tr just made, 3 dc around same tr, repeat from † to † across to last tr, 3 dc around last tr, work ending Split tr, remove marker, working **behind** ending Split tr just made, 3 dc around same tr; join with slip st to top of beginning ch-4, finish off: 402 dc and 66 Split tr.

Rnd 2: With **right** side facing, join Blue with slip st in center dc on either end; ch 3 **(counts as first dc, now and throughout)**, dc in same st, 2 dc in each of next 4 dc, † skip next Split tr, dc in next 3 dc, work Split tr Cluster, working **behind** Split tr Cluster just made, dc in 3 skipped dc †, repeat from † to † across first side, skip next Split tr, 2 dc in each of next 9 dc, repeat from † to † across to last 4 dc, 2 dc in each of last 4 dc; join with slip st to first dc, finish off: 420 dc and 64 Split tr Clusters.

Rnd 3: With **right** side facing, join Green with slip st in same st as joining; ch 3, dc in same st, 2 dc in next dc, † dc in next 8 dc, skip next 3 dc, tr in center of next Split tr Cluster, working **behind** tr just made, dc in 3 skipped dc and in next 3 dc, ★ work Split tr Cluster, working **behind** Split tr Cluster just made, dc in 3 skipped dc and in next 3 dc; repeat from ★ across to next 2-dc group, inserting hook from **back** to **front**, tr in center of same st as last Split tr Cluster made, dc in next 8 dc †, 2 dc in each of next 2 dc, repeat from † to † once; join with slip st to first dc, finish off: 490 sts.

Rnd 4: With **right** side facing, join Off-White with slip st in first tr to left of joining; ch 3, dc in next 6 dc, † (dc in center of next Split tr Cluster and in next 6 dc) across to next tr on same side, dc in next tr and in next dc, work FPtr around dc on Rnd 2 **below** next dc, (skip next dc on Rnd 3, dc in next dc, skip next dc on Rnd 2, work FPtr around next dc) twice, skip next dc on Rnd 3, 2 dc in next dc, skip next dc on Rnd 2, work FPtr around next dc, skip next dc on Rnd 3, 2 dc in next dc, work FPtr around next dc on Rnd 2, dc in next 2 dc on Rnd 3, work FPtr around next dc on Rnd 2, 2 dc in next dc on Rnd 3, work FPtr around next dc on Rnd 2, skip next dc on Rnd 3, 2 dc in next dc, (skip next dc on Rnd 2, work FPtr around next dc, skip next dc on Rnd 3, dc in next dc) 3 times †, dc in next tr and in next 6 dc, repeat from † to † once; join with slip st to first dc: 502 sts.

Rnd 5: Working in Back Loops Only *(Fig. 28, page 139)*, slip st in next dc, ch 1, sc in same st and in next 5 dc, work FPhdc around next dc, ★ (sc in next 6 dc, work FPhdc around next dc) across to within one st of next FPtr on same side, place marker around last FPhdc made for joining placement, sc in next dc, work FPhdc around next FPtr, (sc in next dc, ch 2, slip st in top of sc just made, work FPhdc around next FPtr) twice, (sc in next dc, ch 2, slip st in top of sc just made, sc in next dc, work FPhdc around next FPtr) twice, sc in next dc, ch 4, slip st in top of sc just made, sc in next dc, work FPhdc around next FPtr, (sc in next dc, ch 2, slip st in top of sc just made, sc in next dc, work FPhdc around next FPtr) twice, (sc in next dc, ch 2, slip st in top of sc just made, work FPhdc around next FPtr) twice, sc in next dc, work FPhdc around next dc, place marker around last FPhdc made for joining placement; repeat from ★ once **more**; join with slip st to **both** loops of first sc, finish off.

ASSEMBLY

Place two Strips with **wrong** sides together and top edges at the same end. Using Off-White and working through inside loops only, whipstitch Strips together *(Fig. 35a, page 141)*, beginning in first marked FPhdc and ending in next marked FPhdc.

Join remaining Strips in same manner, always working in same direction.

DREAMY SHELLS Continued from page 60.

Rnd 3: Ch 1, sc in same st, (6 dc in next ch-5 sp, sc in next sc) twice, (work Shell in next ch-3 sp, sc in next sc) across to next ch-5 sp, 6 dc in ch-5 sp, sc in next sc, 6 dc in next ch-5 sp, (sc in next sc, work Shell in next ch-3 sp) across; join with slip st to first sc, finish off.

ASSEMBLY

Place two Strips with **wrong** sides together and bottom edges at the same end. Working through inside loops only and only in Shells along sides, skip first dc of first Shell and join yarn with slip st in next dc; slip st in next 2 dc, (ch 2, skip next 3 sts, slip st in next 3 dc) across; finish off.

Join remaining Strips in same manner, always working in same direction

UNITED IN LOVE Continued from page 62.

ONE-SIDE JOINING

Rnd 2 (Joining rnd)**:** Ch 6, sc in third ch from hook, dc in same st, ch 1, (dc, work Picot, dc) in next dc, place marker around last Picot made for bottom joining, ch 1, [(dc, work Picot, dc) in next dc, ch 1] 5 times, place marker around last Picot made for side joining, [(dc, work Picot, dc) in next dc, ch 1] 7 times, dc in next dc, ch 1, holding Motifs with **wrong** sides together, sc in Picot marked for side joining on **adjacent Motif**, remove marker, ch 1, sc in last ch on **new Motif**, dc in same st as last dc, ch 1, ★ dc in next dc, ch 1, sc in next Picot on **adjacent Motif**, ch 1, sc in last ch on **new Motif**, dc in same st as last dc, ch 1; repeat from ★ once **more**, [(dc, work Picot, dc) in next dc, ch 1] around; join with slip st to first dc, finish off.

TWO-SIDE JOINING

Rnd 2 (Joining rnd)**:** Ch 6, sc in third ch from hook, dc in same st, ch 1, (dc, work Picot, dc) in next dc, place marker around last Picot made for bottom joining, ch 1, [(dc, work Picot, dc) in next dc, ch 1] 5 times, place marker around last Picot made for side joining, [(dc, work Picot, dc) in next dc, ch 1] twice, dc in next dc, ch 1, holding Motifs with **wrong** sides together, sc in Picot marked for bottom joining on **adjacent Motif**, remove marker, ch 1, sc in last ch on **new Motif**, dc in same st as last dc, ch 1, † dc in next dc, ch 1, sc in next Picot on **adjacent Motif**, ch 1, sc in last ch on **new Motif**, dc in same st as last dc, ch 1 †, repeat from † to † once **more**, [(dc, work Picot, dc) in next dc, ch 1] twice, dc in next dc, ch 1, sc in Picot marked for side joining on **adjacent Motif**, remove marker, ch 1, sc in last ch on **new Motif**, dc in same st as last dc, ch 1, repeat from † to † twice, [(dc, work Picot, dc) in next dc, ch 1] around; join with slip st to first dc, finish off.

FILL-IN MOTIF

With White, ch 6; join with slip st to form a ring.

Rnd 1 (Right side)**:** Ch 2, 15 hdc in ring; join with slip st to first hdc: 16 hdc.

Note: Mark Rnd 1 as **right** side.

Rnd 2: Slip st in next hdc and in each hdc around; join with slip st to first slip st.

Rnd 3: Ch 1, working **behind** slip sts and in hdc on Rnd 1, sc in same st and in each hdc around; join with slip st to first sc.

Rnd 4 (Joining rnd)**:** Ch 4 (**counts as first dc plus ch 1, now and throughout**); with **right** side of Afghan facing and working in any intersection of 4 Motifs, sc in any joining, ch 1, dc in same st on **Fill-in Motif**, ch 1, sc in next sc, ch 1, (sc in next Picot on **adjacent Motif**, ch 1, sc in next sc on **Fill-in Motif**, ch 1) twice, ★ dc in next sc, ch 1, sc in next joining, ch 1, dc in same st on **Fill-in Motif**, ch 1, sc in next sc, ch 1, (sc in next Picot on **adjacent Motif**, ch 1, sc in next sc on **Fill-in Motif**, ch 1) twice; repeat from ★ around; join with slip st to first dc, finish off.

Repeat for each space between joined Motifs.

EDGING

With **right** side facing, join White with slip st in first ch-1 sp on first Motif to **left** of any corner Motif; ch 4, [(dc, work Picot, dc) in next ch-1 sp, ch 1] 6 times, dc in next ch-1 sp, ★ † skip next joining, dc in next ch-1 sp, ch 1, [(dc, work Picot, dc) in next ch-1 sp, ch 1] 6 times, dc in next ch-1 sp †, repeat from † to † across to last joining on same side, skip joining, dc in next ch-1 sp, ch 1, [(dc, work Picot, dc) in next ch-1 sp, ch 1] 11 times, dc in next ch-1 sp; repeat from ★ around; join with slip st to first dc, finish off.

DAD'S COMFY WRAP Continued from page 64.

SQUARE ASSEMBLY

Using Tan and working through inside loops only, whipstitch Squares together, forming 5 vertical strips of 9 Squares each *(Fig. 35a, page 141)*, beginning in center sc of first corner 5-sc group and ending in center sc of next corner 5-sc group; do **not** join strips.

STRIP EDGING

Rnd 1: With **right** side facing and working in Back Loops Only, join Cream with slip st in center sc of upper right corner 5-sc group; ch 3, 2 dc in same st, ✝ dc in each sc across to center sc of next corner 5-sc group, 3 dc in center sc, dc in next 22 sc, (dc in same st as joining on same Square and in same st as joining on next Square, dc in next 22 sc) across to center sc of next corner 5-sc group ✝, 3 dc in center sc, repeat from ✝ to ✝ once; join with slip st to first dc: 484 dc.

Rnd 2: Ch 3, working in both loops, 3 dc in next dc, dc in each dc around working 3 dc in center dc of each corner 3-dc group; join with slip st to first dc, finish off: 492 dc.

Rnd 3: With **right** side facing, join Tan with sc in any dc; sc in each dc around working 2 sc in each of 3 corner dc; join with slip st to first sc, finish off: 504 sc.

STRIP ASSEMBLY

Place two strips with **wrong** sides together. Using Tan and working through inside loops only, whipstitch strips together, beginning in first sc **after** three 2-sc groups of first corner and ending in last sc **before** three 2-sc groups of next corner.

BORDER

Rnd 1: With **right** side facing, join Tan with sc in first sc of first corner 2-sc group at upper right corner; [ch 3, (skip next sc, sc in next sc, ch 3) 16 times, (skip next sc, sc in next sc) twice] 4 times, ch 3, (skip next sc, sc in next sc, ch 3) 142 times, (skip next sc, sc in next sc) twice, [ch 3, (skip next sc, sc in next sc, ch 3) 16 times, (skip next sc, sc in next sc) twice] 3 times, ch 3, skip next sc, (sc in next sc, ch 3, skip next sc) around; join with slip st to first sc: 388 ch-3 sps.

Rnd 2: Slip st in next ch-3 sp, ch 1, sc in same sp, [ch 4, (sc in next ch-3 sp, ch 4) 15 times, sc in next 2 ch-3 sps] 4 times, ch 4, (sc in next ch-3 sp, ch 4) 141 times, sc in next 2 ch-3 sps, [ch 4, (sc in next ch-3 sp, ch 4) 15 times, sc in next 2 ch-3 sps] 3 times, ch 4, (sc in next ch-3 sp, ch 4) around; join with slip st to first sc, finish off.

ROCK-A-BYE ROSES Continued from page 66.

Rnds 7 and 8: Ch 1, sc in same sp, (ch 6, sc in next ch-6 sp) around, ch 3, dc in first sc to form last ch-6 sp.

Rnds 9 and 10: Repeat Rnds 6 and 7.

Rnd 11: Ch 1, sc in same sp, ch 6, sc in third ch from hook, ch 3, ★ sc in next ch-6 sp, ch 6, sc in third ch from hook, ch 3; repeat from ★ around; join with slip st to first sc, finish off.

ROSE (Make 6)

With Pink, ch 5; join with slip st to form a ring.

Rnd 1 (Right side): Ch 1, (sc, ch 3) 6 times in ring; join with slip st to first sc: 6 ch-3 sps.

Note: Mark Rnd 1 as **right** side.

Rnd 2: Slip st in first ch-3 sp, ch 1, (sc, 4 dc, sc) in same sp and in each ch-3 sp around; join with slip st to first sc: 6 petals.

Rnd 3: Ch 1, working **behind** petals and around skipped sc on Rnd 1, work BPsc around first sc, ch 4, (work BPsc around next sc, ch 4) around; join with slip st to first BPsc: 6 ch-4 sps.

Rnd 4: Slip st in first ch-4 sp, ch 1, (sc, 6 dc, sc) in same sp and in each ch-4 sp around; join with slip st to first sc, finish off.

LEAF (Make 8)

With Green, ch 10 **loosely**.

Row 1 (Right side): Sc in second ch from hook and in next 7 chs, 3 sc in last ch; working in free loops of beginning ch, sc in next 8 chs: 19 sc.

Note: Mark Row 1 as **right** side.

Row 2: Ch 1, turn; sc in Back Loops Only of first 7 sc *(Fig. 28, page 139)*, leave remaining 12 sc unworked: 7 sc.

Row 3: Ch 1, turn; working in Back Loops Only, sc in first 7 sc, 3 sc in beginning ch, sc in next 7 sc, leave remaining 5 sc unworked: 17 sc.

Row 4: Ch 1, turn; working in Back Loops Only, sc in first 7 sc, 2 sc in each of next 2 sc, sc in next 6 sc, leave remaining 2 sc unworked.

Row 5: Ch 1, turn; working in Back Loops Only, sc in first 5 sc, 2 sc in next sc, sc in next 3 sc, 2 sc in next sc, sc in next 5 sc, leave remaining 2 sc unworked; finish off.

Using photo as a guide for placement, sew Roses and Leaves to opposite corners of Afghan.

July

AMERICAN RIPPLE

Bursting with patriotic pride, this ripple afghan is an all-American accent for Independence Day. Glorious waves of red, blue, and ecru are accented by clusters and chain spaces.

Finished Size: 48" x 61"

MATERIALS
Worsted Weight Yarn:
 Dk Blue - 3 ounces,
  (90 grams, 195 yards)
 Blue - 8 ounces,
  (230 grams, 525 yards)
 Tan - 10 ounces,
  (280 grams, 655 yards)
 Ecru - 8 ounces,
  (230 grams, 525 yards)
 Red - 6 ounces,
  (170 grams, 395 yards)
Crochet hook, size H (5.00 mm) **or** size
 needed for gauge

GAUGE: One repeat from point to point
 and 8 rows = 6"

Gauge Swatch: 12"w x 6"h
Ch 61 **loosely**.
Work same as Afghan for 8 rows.
Finish off.

STITCH GUIDE

3-DC CLUSTER (uses next 3 sts)
★ YO, insert hook in **next** st or ch, YO and pull up a loop, YO and draw through 2 loops on hook; repeat from ★ 2 times **more**, YO and draw through all 4 loops on hook *(Figs. 17c & d, page 136)*.

5-DC CLUSTER (uses next 5 sts)
★ YO, insert hook in **next** st or ch, YO and pull up a loop, YO and draw through 2 loops on hook; repeat from ★ 4 times **more**, YO and draw through all 6 loops on hook.

COLOR SEQUENCE

One row **each**: Dk Blue, ★ Blue, Tan, Ecru, Red, Ecru, Tan, Blue, Dk Blue; repeat from ★ throughout.

With Dk Blue, ch 229 **loosely**.

Row 1 (Right side): YO, insert hook in fourth ch from hook **(3 skipped chs count as first dc)**, YO and pull up a loop, YO and draw through 2 loops on hook, (YO, insert hook in **next** ch, YO and pull up a loop, YO and draw through 2 loops on hook) twice, YO and draw through all 4 loops on hook, dc in next 11 chs, 5 dc in next ch, dc in next 11 chs, ★ work 5-dc Cluster, dc in next 11 chs, 5 dc in next ch, dc in next 11 chs; repeat from ★ across to last 4 chs, work 3-dc Cluster, dc in last ch: 227 sts.

Row 2: Ch 3 **(counts as first dc, now and throughout)**, turn; working in both loops, work 3-dc Cluster, ch 1, (skip next dc, dc in next dc, ch 1) 5 times, skip next dc, 5 dc in next dc, ch 1, (skip next dc, dc in next dc, ch 1) 5 times, ★ skip next dc, work 5-dc Cluster, ch 1, (skip next dc, dc in next dc, ch 1) 5 times, skip next dc, 5 dc in next dc, ch 1, (skip next dc, dc in next dc, ch 1) 5 times; repeat from ★ across to last 5 sts, skip next dc, work 3-dc Cluster, dc in last dc: 131 sts and 96 ch-1 sps.

Row 3: Ch 3, turn; working in Back Loops Only of sts and in chs *(Fig. 28, page 139)*, work 3-dc Cluster, dc in next 11 sts, 5 dc in next dc, dc in next 11 sts, ★ work 5-dc Cluster, dc in next 11 sts, 5 dc in next dc, dc in next 11 sts; repeat from ★ across to last 4 sts, work 3-dc Cluster, dc in last dc: 227 sts.

Repeat Rows 2 and 3 until Afghan measures 61" from beginning ch, ending by working one row Dk Blue.
Finish off.

STAR-SPANGLED SALUTE

Stitched using a jumbo hook and holding two strands of yarn together, this bold afghan works up quickly for a star-spangled salute to freedom. Each block shines with a simple four-pointed star set against a deep blue background. The squares are easily assembled in strips and edged with a single crochet border.

Finished Size: 53" x 64"

MATERIALS

Worsted Weight Yarn:

Navy - 30 ounces, (850 grams, 1,885 yards)

Ecru - 21½ ounces, (610 grams, 1,350 yards)

Crochet hook, size Q (15.00 mm)

Yarn needle

GAUGE: 12 sc and 14 rows = 8"

Each Block = 17"w x 15½"h

Note: Entire Afghan is worked holding two strands of yarn together.

BLOCK (Make 12)

With Navy, ch 27 **loosely**.

Row 1 (Right side): Sc in second ch from hook and in each ch across: 26 sc.

Note: Loop a short piece of yarn around any stitch to mark Row 1 as **right** side and bottom edge.

Row 2: Ch 1, turn; sc in first 18 sc changing to Ecru in last sc *(Fig. 31a, page 139)*, sc in next sc changing to Navy, sc in last 7 sc.

Row 3: Ch 1, turn; sc in first 7 sc, with Ecru sc in next 2 sc, with Navy sc in last 17 sc.

Row 4: Ch 1, turn; sc in first 16 sc, with Ecru sc in next 3 sc, with Navy sc in last 7 sc.

Row 5: Ch 1, turn; sc in first 7 sc, with Ecru sc in next 4 sc, with Navy sc in last 15 sc.

Row 6: Ch 1, turn; sc in first 14 sc, with Ecru sc in next 5 sc, with Navy sc in last 7 sc.

Row 7: Ch 1, turn; sc in first 7 sc, with Ecru sc in next 6 sc, with Navy sc in last 13 sc.

Row 8: Ch 1, turn; sc in first sc, with Ecru sc in next 18 sc, with Navy sc in last 7 sc.

Row 9: Ch 1, turn; sc in first 7 sc, with Ecru sc in next 17 sc, with Navy sc in last 2 sc.

Row 10: Ch 1, turn; sc in first 3 sc, with Ecru sc in next 16 sc, with Navy sc in last 7 sc.

Row 11: Ch 1, turn; sc in first 7 sc, with Ecru sc in next 15 sc, with Navy sc in last 4 sc.

Row 12: Ch 1, turn; sc in first 5 sc, with Ecru sc in next 14 sc, with Navy sc in last 7 sc.

Rows 13 and 14: Ch 1, turn; sc in first 7 sc, with Ecru sc in next 13 sc, with Navy sc in last 6 sc.

Row 15: Repeat Row 12.

Row 16: Repeat Row 11.

Row 17: Repeat Row 10.

Row 18: Repeat Row 9.

Row 19: Repeat Row 8.

Row 20: Repeat Row 7.

Row 21: Repeat Row 6.

Row 22: Repeat Row 5.

Row 23: Repeat Row 4.

Row 24: Repeat Row 3.

Row 25: Ch 1, turn; sc in first 18 sc, with Ecru sc in next sc, cut Ecru, with Navy sc in last 7 sc.

Row 26: Ch 1, turn; sc in each sc across; finish off.

ASSEMBLY

With **right** sides facing and Navy, sew Blocks together, forming 3 vertical strips of 4 Blocks each, matching bottom edge of one Block to top edge of next Block; sew strips together in same manner.

EDGING

Rnd 1: With **right** side facing, join Ecru with sc in any corner sc *(see Joining With Sc, page 139)*; 2 sc in same st, sc evenly around working 3 sc in each corner; join with slip st to first sc, finish off.

Rnd 2: With **right** side facing, join Navy with sc in any corner sc; 2 sc in same st, sc evenly around working 3 sc in each corner; join with slip st to first sc, finish off.

SUMMER SUNRISE

Greet a summer sunrise wrapped in this softly colored throw that reflects the morning light. Each mile-a-minute strip is created with rings of yellow and blue that are linked together as you go.

Finished Size: 48" x 69"

MATERIALS

Worsted Weight Yarn:
  Yellow - 26 ounces, (740 grams, 1,710 yards)
  Blue - 24 ounces, (680 grams, 1,575 yards)
  Ecru - 15 ounces, (430 grams, 985 yards)
Crochet hook, size G (4.00 mm) **or** size needed
  for gauge
Yarn needle

GAUGE: 16 dc and 8 rows = 4"
        Each Ring = 2¹/₂" in diameter
        Each Strip = 4¹/₄" wide

STITCH GUIDE

> **DECREASE**
> Pull up a loop in next st on **same Strip** and in next st on **next Strip**, YO and draw through all 3 loops on hook.

STRIP (Make 11)

CENTER

FIRST RING

With Yellow, ch 15; join with slip st to form a ring.

Rnd 1 (Right side)**:** Ch 3 **(counts as first dc, now and throughout)**, 29 dc in ring; join with slip st to first dc, finish off: 30 dc.

Note: Loop a short piece of yarn around any stitch to mark Rnd 1 as **right** side.

SECOND RING

With Blue, ch 15, with **wrong** side of previous Ring facing, insert end of beginning ch-15 through center of previous Ring; join with slip st to form a ring.

Rnd 1 (Right side)**:** Ch 3, 29 dc in ring; join with slip st to first dc, finish off: 30 dc.

Note: Mark Rnd 1 as **right** side.

THIRD RING

With Yellow, ch 15, with **wrong** side of previous Ring facing, insert end of beginning ch-15 through center of previous Ring; join with slip st to form a ring.

Rnd 1 (Right side)**:** Ch 3, 29 dc in ring; join with slip st to first dc, finish off: 30 dc.

Note: Mark Rnd 1 as **right** side.

REMAINING 46 RINGS

Repeat Second and Third Rings, 23 times: 49 Rings.

BORDER

Note: Work into Rings with **right** side of each Ring facing you at all times.

Rnd 1: With **right** side facing, join Ecru with slip st in any dc on First Ring; ch 3, dc in next 4 dc, ch 2, dc in next 7 dc on same Ring, ch 2, dc in next 5 dc on same Ring, ch 2, (dc in any 5 consecutive dc on next Ring, ch 2) 48 times, dc in next 7 dc on same Ring, ch 2, dc in next 5 dc on same Ring, ch 2, (skip next 10 dc on next Ring, dc in next 5 dc, ch 2) across; join with slip st to first dc: 504 dc and 100 ch-2 sps.

Rnd 2: Ch 1, sc in same st and in next 4 dc, 2 sc in next ch-2 sp, sc in next 7 dc, 2 sc in next ch-2 sp, sc in next 5 dc, (sc in next ch-2 sp and in next 5 dc) 48 times, 2 sc in next ch-2 sp, sc in next 7 dc, 2 sc in next ch-2 sp, (sc in next 5 dc and in next ch-2 sp) across changing to Yellow in last sc *(Fig. 31a, page 139)*; join with slip st to Back Loop Only of first sc *(Fig. 28, page 139)*: 608 sc.

Rnd 3: Ch 1, working in Back Loops Only, sc in same st, † place marker around sc just made for joining placement, sc in next 5 sc, 2 sc in each of next 9 sc, sc in next 6 sc, place marker around last sc made for joining placement †, sc in next 284 sc, repeat from † to † once, sc in each sc across; join with slip st to both loops of first sc, finish off.

ASSEMBLY

Place two Strips with **wrong** sides together. Using Yellow and working through inside loops only, whipstitch Strips together *(Fig. 35a, page 141)*, beginning in first marked sc and ending in next marked sc.

Join remaining Strips in same manner, always working in same direction.

EDGING

With **right** side facing and working in Back Loops Only, join Blue with sc in marked sc at top of first Strip *(see Joining With Sc, page 139)*, remove all markers; sc in next 7 sc, † 2 sc in next sc, sc in next 3 sc, 2 sc in next sc, sc in next 4 sc, 2 sc in next sc, sc in next 3 sc, 2 sc in next sc, ★ sc in next 6 sc, decrease, sc in next 6 sc, 2 sc in next sc, sc in next 3 sc, 2 sc in next sc, sc in next 4 sc, 2 sc in next sc, sc in next 3 sc, 2 sc in next sc; repeat from ★ 9 times **more** †, sc in next 299 sc, repeat from † to † once, sc in each sc across; join with slip st to both loops of first sc, finish off.

SEASHELL BASKETS

This delicate afghan features a collection of fanciful "shells" that recalls the ocean treasures we love to gather along the shore. The seaside throw makes an ideal accent for a summer beach house.

Finished Size: 46" x 69"

MATERIALS
Worsted Weight Yarn:
    40 ounces, (1,140 grams, 2,745 yards)
Crochet hook, size H (5.00 mm) **or** size needed
    for gauge

GAUGE SWATCH: 6¹/₂"w x 6"h
Ch 25 **loosely**.
Work same as Afghan for 11 rows.
Finish off.

STITCH GUIDE

> **SHELL**
> (Sc, ch 2, dc) in dc indicated.

Ch 151 **loosely**.
Row 1 (Right side): Dc in fourth ch from hook **(3 skipped chs count as first dc)** and in each ch across: 149 dc.
Note: Loop a short piece of yarn around any stitch to mark Row 1 as **right** side.
Row 2: Ch 3 **(counts as first dc, now and throughout)**, turn; dc in next dc, ★ ch 1, skip next dc, dc in next dc; repeat from ★ across to last 3 dc, ch 1, skip next dc, dc in last 2 dc: 76 dc and 73 ch-1 sps.
Row 3: Ch 3, turn; dc in next dc, ch 1, ★ skip next ch-1 sp, dc in next dc, (dc in next ch-1 sp and in next dc) 8 times, ch 1; repeat from ★ across to last 2 dc, dc in last 2 dc: 140 dc and 9 ch-1 sps.
Row 4: Ch 3, turn; dc in next dc, ch 1, ★ dc in next 7 dc, skip next dc, (tr, ch 3, tr) in next dc, skip next dc, dc in next 7 dc, ch 1; repeat from ★ across to last 2 dc, dc in last 2 dc: 132 sts and 17 sps.
Row 5: Ch 3, turn; dc in next dc, ch 1, dc in next 5 dc, ch 1, 6 dc in next ch-3 sp, ch 1, ★ skip next 3 sts, (dc in next 5 dc, ch 1) twice, 6 dc in next ch-3 sp, ch 1; repeat from ★ across to last 10 sts, skip next 3 sts, dc in next 5 dc, ch 1, dc in last 2 dc: 132 dc.
Row 6: Ch 3, turn; dc in next dc, ch 1, dc in next 4 dc, ch 1, skip next dc, (dc in next dc, ch 1) 6 times, ★ skip next dc, (dc in next 4 dc, ch 1) twice, skip next dc, (dc in next dc, ch 1) 6 times; repeat from ★ across to last 7 dc, skip next dc, dc in next 4 dc, ch 1, dc in last 2 dc: 116 dc.

Row 7: Ch 3, turn; dc in next dc, ch 1, dc in next 2 dc, ch 1, skip next 2 dc, dc in next dc, (ch 2, dc in next dc) 5 times, ch 1, ★ skip next 2 dc, (dc in next 2 dc, ch 1) twice, skip next 2 dc, dc in next dc, (ch 2, dc in next dc) 5 times, ch 1; repeat from ★ across to last 6 dc, skip next 2 dc, dc in next 2 dc, ch 1, dc in last 2 dc: 84 dc.
Row 8: Ch 3, turn; dc in next dc, ch 1, dc in next 2 dc, ★ ch 2, work Shell in next 5 dc, sc in next dc, ch 2, dc in next 2 dc, ch 1, dc in next 2 dc; repeat from ★ across: 40 Shells.
Row 9: Ch 3, turn; dc in next dc, ch 1, ★ dc in next 2 dc and in next ch-2 sp, ch 1, skip next sc, working **behind** Shells, tr in next ch-2 sp one row **below**, ch 1, (dc in next ch-2 sp one row **below**, ch 1) 3 times, tr in next ch-2 sp one row **below**, ch 1, skip next sc, dc in next ch-2 sp and in next 2 dc, ch 1; repeat from ★ across to last 2 dc, dc in last 2 dc: 92 sts and 57 ch-1 sps.
Row 10: Ch 3, turn; dc in next dc, ch 1, ★ dc in next 3 dc and in next ch-1 sp, (dc in next st and in next ch-1 sp) 5 times, dc in next 3 dc, ch 1; repeat from ★ across to last 2 dc, dc in last 2 dc: 140 dc and 9 ch-1 sps.
Row 11: Ch 3, turn; dc in next dc, ch 1, (dc in next 17 dc, ch 1) across to last 2 dc, dc in last 2 dc.
Row 12: Ch 3, turn; (dc in next dc, ch 1) twice, (skip next dc, dc in next dc, ch 1) 8 times, ★ dc in next dc, ch 1, (skip next dc, dc in next dc, ch 1) 8 times; repeat from ★ across to last 2 dc, dc in last 2 dc: 76 dc and 73 ch-1 sps.
Rows 13-122: Repeat Rows 3-12, 11 times: 76 dc and 73 ch-1 sps.
Row 123: Ch 3, turn; dc in each dc and each ch-1 sp across; do **not** finish off: 149 dc.

EDGING

Rnd 1: Ch 1, do **not** turn; sc in last dc on Row 123, ch 1; working in end of rows, skip first row, (sc in next row, ch 1) across; working in free loops of beginning ch *(Fig. 29b, page 139)*, (sc, ch 2, sc) in first ch, ch 1, (skip next ch, sc in next ch, ch 1) 73 times, skip next ch, (sc, ch 2, sc) in next ch, ch 1; working in end of rows, skip first row, (sc in next row, ch 1) across; working across sts on Row 123, (sc, ch 2, sc) in first dc, ch 1, (skip next dc, sc in next dc, ch 1) 73 times, skip next dc, sc in same st as first dc, ch 2; join with slip st to first sc: 398 sps.

Rnd 2: Slip st in first ch-1 sp, ch 4 **(counts as first dc plus ch 1, now and throughout)**, ★ (dc in next ch-1 sp, ch 1) across to next corner ch-2 sp, (dc, ch 3, dc) in corner ch-2 sp, ch 1; repeat from ★ around; join with slip st to first dc: 402 dc.

Rnd 3: Ch 4, ★ (dc in next dc, ch 1) across to next corner ch-3 sp, (dc, ch 3, dc) in corner ch-3 sp, ch 1; repeat from ★ around to last dc, dc in last dc, ch 1; join with slip st to first dc: 410 sps.

Rnd 4: Slip st in first ch-1 sp, ch 2, ★ (slip st in next ch-1 sp, ch 2) across to next corner ch-3 sp, (slip st, ch 2) twice in corner ch-3 sp; repeat from ★ around to last 2 ch-1 sps, (slip st in next ch-1 sp, ch 2) twice; join with slip st to first slip st, finish off.

BABY'S CHOICE

Strips of clusters worked in tranquil pastels are bordered with white to create this bonny wrap for baby. The sport weight throw will make a "beary" sweet choice for your favorite little one.

STITCH GUIDE

3-TR CLUSTER
Ch 4, ★ YO twice, insert hook in fourth ch from hook, YO and pull up a loop, (YO and draw through 2 loops on hook) twice; repeat from ★ 2 times **more**, YO and draw through all 4 loops on hook *(Figs. 17a & b, page 136)*.

4-TR CLUSTER
★ YO twice, insert hook in st indicated, YO and pull up a loop, (YO and draw through 2 loops on hook) twice; repeat from ★ 3 times **more**, YO and draw through all 5 loops on hook.

STRIP (Make 15)

Note: The color used for the Foundation Row and Rnd 1 varies. Work the Foundation Row and Rnd 1 in the color specified for the number of Strips indicated: Aqua - 3, Purple - 2, Pink - 2, Blue - 2, Green - 2, Yellow - 2, and Peach - 2.

Foundation Row (Right side)**:** Work 56 3-tr Clusters.
Note: Loop a short piece of yarn around last 3-tr Cluster made to mark top edge and to mark Foundation Row as **right** side.
Rnd 1: Ch 5, work 4-tr Cluster at base of first Cluster, (ch 3, work 4-tr Cluster at base of next Cluster) across to last Cluster, ch 5, slip st in base of last Cluster, ch 5, work 4-tr Cluster at base of next Cluster, (ch 3, work 4-tr Cluster at base of next Cluster) across, ch 5; join with slip st to base of beginning ch-5, finish off: 110 4-tr Clusters and 112 sps.
Rnd 2: With **right** side facing, join White with slip st in first ch-5 sp to right of joining; ch 3 (**counts as first dc**), (2 dc, 7 tr) in same sp, 3 tr in next slip st, (7 tr, 3 dc) in next ch-5 sp, 4 dc in each ch-3 sp across to next ch-5 sp, (3 dc, 7 tr) in ch-5 sp, 3 tr in next slip st, (7 tr, 3 dc) in next ch-5 sp, 4 dc in each ch-3 sp across; join with slip st to first dc, finish off: 478 sts.

Finished Size: 31" x 41"

MATERIALS
Sport Weight Yarn:
White - 6³/₄ ounces,
(190 grams, 755 yards)
Aqua - 2¹/₂ ounces,
(70 grams, 280 yards)
Purple, Pink, Blue, Green, Yellow,
and Peach - 1¹/₂ ounces,
(40 grams, 170 yards) **each**
Crochet hook, size E (3.50 mm) **or** size needed for gauge

GAUGE: Each Strip = 2" wide
7 3-tr Clusters on Foundation
Row = 5"

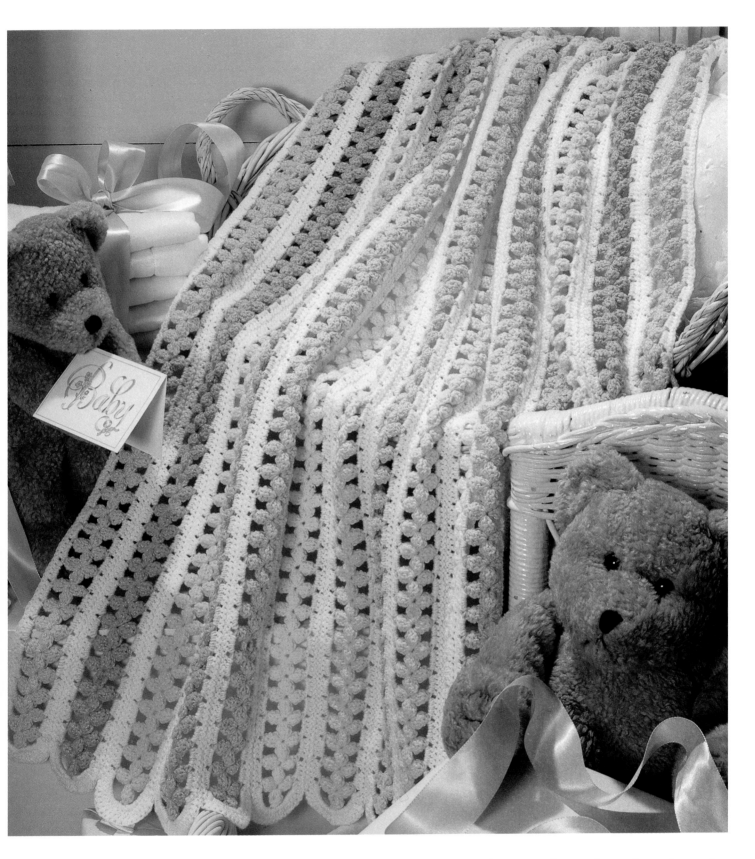

ASSEMBLY

Afghan is assembled by joining Strips in the following color sequence: Aqua, Purple, Pink, Blue, Green, Yellow, Peach, Aqua, Peach, Yellow, Green, Blue, Pink, Purple, and Aqua.

Place two Strips with **wrong** sides together and top edges at the same end. Using White and working through both loops of each stitch on **both** pieces, slip st in first dc on side of Strip; ch 1, sc in same st and in each dc across; finish off.

Join remaining Strips in same manner, always working in same direction.

OCEAN WAVES

The ripples in this maritime throw resemble white-capped waves on a sun-kissed sea. Treble crochets and clusters give the worsted weight beauty its unusual texture.

Finished Size: 51" x 72"

MATERIALS

Worsted Weight Yarn:
  Off-White - 19 ounces, (540 grams, 1,305 yards)
  Dk Teal - 15 ounces, (430 grams, 1,030 yards)
  Teal - 15 ounces, (430 grams, 1,030 yards)
  Crochet hook, size I (5.50 mm) **or** size needed for gauge

GAUGE: In pattern, 2 repeats = 8½"
  and 8 rows = 4½"

Gauge Swatch: 9"w x 4½"h
Ch 43 **loosely**.
Work same as Afghan for 8 rows.

STITCH GUIDE

> **CLUSTER**
> Ch 3, ★ YO, insert hook in third ch from hook, YO and pull up a loop, YO and draw through 2 loops on hook; repeat from ★ once **more**, YO and draw through all 3 loops on hook (*Figs. 17a & b, page 136*).

COLOR SEQUENCE

2 Rows Off-White, 1 row **each**: Dk Teal, Teal, Dk Teal, ★ Off-White, Teal, Dk Teal, Teal, Off-White, Dk Teal, Teal, Dk Teal; repeat from ★ 14 times **more**, then work 2 rows Off-White.

With Off-White, ch 233 **loosely**.

Row 1: Sc in second ch from hook, ch 3, skip next 2 chs, sc in next ch, ★ (ch 1, skip next ch, sc in next ch) 8 times, ch 3, skip next 2 chs, sc in next ch; repeat from ★ across: 110 sc and 109 sps.

Row 2 (Right side)**:** Ch 5 **(counts as first tr plus ch 1, now and throughout)**, turn; (dc, ch 1) twice in next ch-3 sp, tr in next 9 sc, ch 1, ★ (dc, ch 1, dc, ch 3, dc, ch 1, dc) in next ch-3 sp, ch 1, tr in next 9 sc, ch 1; repeat from ★ across to last ch-3 sp, (dc, ch 1) twice in ch-3 sp, tr in last sc; finish off: 158 sts and 61 sps.

Note: Loop a short piece of yarn around any stitch to mark Row 2 as **right** side.

Row 3: With **wrong** side facing, join next color with sc in first tr *(see Joining With Sc, page 139)*; ch 3, (sc in next dc, ch 1) twice, sc in next tr, (ch 1, skip next tr, sc in next tr) 4 times, (ch 1, sc in next dc) twice, ★ work Cluster, (sc in next dc, ch 1) twice, sc in next tr, (ch 1, skip next tr, sc in next tr) 4 times, (ch 1, sc in next dc) twice; repeat from ★ across to last tr, ch 3, sc in last tr; finish off: 11 Clusters.

Row 4: With **right** side facing, join next color with slip st in first sc; ch 5, (dc, ch 1) twice in next ch-3 sp, tr in next 9 sc, ch 1, ★ working **behind** next Cluster, (tr, ch 1, tr, ch 3, tr, ch 1, tr) in ch-3 sp one row **below** Cluster, ch 1, tr in next 9 sc, ch 1; repeat from ★ across to last ch-3 sp, (dc, ch 1) twice in ch-3 sp, tr in last sc; finish off: 158 sts and 61 sps.

Row 5: With **wrong** side facing, join next color with sc in first tr; ch 3, (sc in next dc, ch 1) twice, sc in next tr, (ch 1, skip next tr, sc in next tr) 4 times, (ch 1, sc in next tr) twice, work Cluster, ★ † sc in next tr, (ch 1, sc in next tr) twice, (ch 1, skip next tr, sc in next tr) 4 times †, (ch 1, sc in next tr) twice, work Cluster; repeat from ★ 9 times **more**, then repeat from † to † once, (ch 1, sc in next dc) twice, ch 3, sc in last tr; finish off: 11 Clusters.

Rows 6-125: Repeat Rows 4 and 5, 60 times.

Row 126: With **right** side facing, join Off-White with slip st in first sc; ch 5, (dc, ch 1) twice in next ch-3 sp, tr in next 9 sc, ch 1, ★ working **behind** next Cluster, (tr, ch 1) 4 times in ch-3 sp one row **below** Cluster, tr in next 9 sc, ch 1; repeat from ★ across to last ch-3 sp, (dc, ch 1) twice in ch-3 sp, tr in last sc: 158 sts and 61 sps.

Row 127: Ch 1, turn; sc in first tr, ch 1, (sc in next dc, ch 1) twice, sc in next tr, (ch 1, skip next tr, sc in next tr) 4 times, ch 1, (sc in next tr, ch 1) twice, sc in next ch-1 sp, ★ † ch 1, (sc in next tr, ch 1) 3 times, (skip next tr, sc in next tr, ch 1) 4 times †, (sc in next tr, ch 1) twice, sc in next ch-1 sp; repeat from ★ 9 times **more**, then repeat from † to † once, (sc in next dc, ch 1) twice, sc in last tr; finish off.

RIPPLING EFFECTS

Ripples and cables combine to make this throw pretty in pink.
It's crocheted using a combination of pattern stitches,
including clusters and front and back post treble crochets.

Finished Size: 49" x 63"

MATERIALS

Worsted Weight Yarn:
Dk Pink - 13 ounces, (370 grams, 965 yards)
Pink - 11 ounces, (310 grams, 815 yards)
Lt Pink - 12 ounces, (340 grams, 890 yards)
Crochet hook, size H (5.00 mm) **or** size needed
for gauge

GAUGE: One repeat from point to point = 7¼"
and 6 rows = 4¼"

Gauge Swatch: 12¼"w x 4¼"h
Ch 54 **loosely**.
Work same as Afghan for 6 rows.
Finish off.

STITCH GUIDE

CLUSTER
★ YO, insert hook in **next** st, YO and pull up a loop, YO and
draw through 2 loops on hook; repeat from ★ 2 times **more**,
YO and draw through all 4 loops on hook *(Figs. 17c & d,
page 136)*.

BACK POST TREBLE CROCHET
(abbreviated BPtr)
YO twice, insert hook from **back** to **front** around post of st
indicated, YO and pull up a loop *(Fig. 16, page 136)*, (YO
and draw through 2 loops on hook) 3 times. Skip st in front
of BPtr.

FRONT POST DOUBLE TREBLE CROCHET
(abbreviated FPdtr)
YO 3 times, insert hook from **front** to **back** around post of st
indicated, YO and pull up a loop *(Fig. 14, page 135)*, (YO
and draw through 2 loops on hook) 4 times. Skip st behind
FPdtr.

CABLE
Skip next 2 BPtr, work FPdtr around each of next 2 BPtr,
working in **front** of 2 FPdtr just made, work FPdtr around
first skipped BPtr and around next skipped BPtr
(Figs. 26a & b, page 138).

COLOR SEQUENCE

4 Rows **each**: Dk Pink *(Fig. 31a, page 139)*, ★ Pink, Lt Pink,
Dk Pink; repeat from ★ throughout.

With Dk Pink, ch 199 **loosely**.
Row 1 (Right side)**:** YO, insert hook in fourth ch from hook
(3 skipped chs count as first dc), YO and pull up a loop, YO
and draw through 2 loops on hook, (YO, insert hook in **next**
ch, YO and pull up a loop, YO and draw through 2 loops on
hook) twice, YO and draw through all 4 loops on hook, dc in
next 7 chs, 5 dc in next ch, dc in next 7 chs, work Cluster, dc in
next ch, ★ ch 1, skip next ch, tr in next ch, skip next ch, 2 tr in
next ch, working around 2 tr just made, 2 tr in skipped ch, tr in
next ch, ch 1, skip next ch, dc in next ch, work Cluster, dc in
next 7 chs, 5 dc in next ch, dc in next 7 chs, work Cluster, dc in
next ch; repeat from ★ across: 197 sts and 12 ch-1 sps.
Row 2: Ch 3 **(counts as first dc, now and throughout)**,
turn; work Cluster, dc in next 7 dc, 5 dc in next dc, dc in next
7 dc, work Cluster, dc in next dc, ★ ch 1, tr in next tr, work BPtr
around each of next 4 tr, tr in next tr, ch 1, dc in next dc, work
Cluster, dc in next 7 dc, 5 dc in next dc, dc in next 7 dc, work
Cluster, dc in next dc; repeat from ★ across.
Row 3: Ch 3, turn; work Cluster, dc in next 7 dc, 5 dc in next
dc, dc in next 7 dc, work Cluster, dc in next dc, ★ ch 1, tr in
next tr, work Cable, tr in next tr, ch 1, dc in next dc, work
Cluster, dc in next 7 dc, 5 dc in next dc, dc in next 7 dc, work
Cluster, dc in next dc; repeat from ★ across.
Row 4: Ch 3, turn; work Cluster, dc in next 7 dc, 5 dc in next
dc, dc in next 7 dc, work Cluster, dc in next dc, ★ ch 1, tr in
next tr, work BPtr around each of next 4 FPdtr, tr in next tr,
ch 1, dc in next dc, work Cluster, dc in next 7 dc, 5 dc in next
dc, dc in next 7 dc, work Cluster, dc in next dc; repeat from ★
across.
Repeat Rows 3 and 4 until Afghan measures 63" from beginning
ch, ending by working 4 rows Dk Pink .
Finish off.

SHELLS IN A NET

Warm weather encourages outings to the beach, where shells are continually discovered along the shoreline. This informal throw was inspired by the treasures often scooped up in a fisherman's netting.

Finished Size: 52" x 71"

MATERIALS
Worsted Weight Yarn:
> 43 ounces, (1,220 grams, 2,825 yards)
> Crochet hook, size H (5.00 mm) **or** size needed
> for gauge

GAUGE SWATCH: 13½"w x 3½"h
Ch 46 **loosely**.
Work same as Afghan for 7 rows.
Finish off.

STITCH GUIDE

> **SHELL**
> 5 Tr in next sc.

Ch 166 **loosely**.

Row 1: Sc in second ch from hook, ★ ch 5, skip next 3 chs, sc in next ch; repeat from ★ across: 41 ch-5 sps.

Row 2 (Right side): Ch 5 **(counts as first dc plus ch 2, now and throughout)**, turn; sc in first ch-5 sp, (ch 5, sc in next ch-5 sp) across to last sc, ch 2, dc in last sc: 40 ch-5 sps.

Row 3: Ch 1, turn; sc in first dc, ch 5, sc in next ch-5 sp, (work Shell, sc in next ch-5 sp) 3 times, ★ (ch 5, sc in next ch-5 sp) 3 times, (work Shell, sc in next ch-5 sp) 3 times; repeat from ★ across to last 2 sts, ch 5, skip next sc, sc in last dc: 21 Shells.

Row 4: Ch 5, turn; sc in first ch-5 sp, ch 5, skip next 3 sts, sc in next tr, (ch 5, skip next 5 sts, sc in next tr) twice, ch 5, ★ (sc in next ch-5 sp, ch 5) 3 times, skip next 3 sts, sc in next tr, ch 5, (skip next 5 sts, sc in next tr, ch 5) twice; repeat from ★ across to last ch-5 sp, sc in last ch-5 sp, ch 2, dc in last sc: 40 ch-5 sps.

Rows 5-8: Repeat Rows 3 and 4 twice.

Row 9: Ch 1, turn; sc in first dc, (ch 5, sc in next ch-5 sp) 4 times, ★ (work Shell, sc in next ch-5 sp) 3 times, (ch 5, sc in next ch-5 sp) 3 times; repeat from ★ across to last 2 sts, ch 5, skip next sc, sc in last dc: 18 Shells.

Row 10: Ch 5, turn; sc in first ch-5 sp, ch 5, ★ (sc in next ch-5 sp, ch 5) 3 times, skip next 3 sts, sc in next tr, ch 5, (skip next 5 sts, sc in next tr, ch 5) twice, (sc in next ch-5 sp, ch 5) 3 times; repeat from ★ across to last ch-5 sp, sc in last ch-5 sp, ch 2, dc in last sc: 40 ch-3 sps.

Rows 11-14: Repeat Rows 9 and 10 twice.

Rows 15-140: Repeat Rows 3-14, 10 times; then repeat Rows 3-8 once **more**.

Row 141: Ch 1, turn; sc in first dc, ch 3, (sc in next ch-5 sp, ch 3) across to last dc, sc in last dc; do **not** finish off: 41 ch-3 sps.

EDGING

Rnd 1: Ch 1, turn; sc in first sc and in next 3 chs, sc in each sc and in each ch across to last sc, (sc, ch 2, sc) in last sc, ch 1; working in end of rows, skip first row, (sc in next row, ch 1) across to last row, skip last row; working in free loops of beginning ch *(Fig. 29b, page 139)*, (sc, ch 2, sc) in ch at base of first sc, sc in each ch across to last ch, (sc, ch 2, sc) in last ch; working in end of rows, skip first row, ch 1, (sc in next row, ch 1) across to last row, skip last row, sc in same st as first sc, ch 2; join with slip st to first sc: 612 sc.

Rnd 2: Ch 1, do **not** turn; sc in same st, ★ sc in each sc across to next corner ch-2 sp, (sc, ch 2, sc) in corner ch-2 sp, sc in next sc, (ch 1, sc in next sc) across to next corner ch-2 sp, (sc, ch 2, sc) in corner ch-2 sp; repeat from ★ once **more**; join with slip st to first sc: 620 sc.

Rnd 3: Ch 1, sc in same st, ch 1, skip next sc, ★ (sc in next sc, ch 1, skip next sc) across to next corner ch-2 sp, (sc, ch 2, sc) in corner ch-2 sp, ch 1, skip next sc, (sc in next sc, ch 1) across to within one sc of next corner ch-2 sp, skip next sc, (sc, ch 2, sc) in corner ch-2 sp, ch 1, skip next sc; repeat from ★ once **more**; join with slip st to first sc.

Rnd 4: Slip st in first ch-1 sp, ★ (ch 2, slip st in next ch-1 sp) across to next corner ch-2 sp, (ch 2, slip st) twice in corner ch-2 sp, ch 1, (slip st in next ch-1 sp, ch 1) across to next corner ch-2 sp, (slip st, ch 2, slip st) in corner ch-2 sp; repeat from ★ once **more**, ch 2, slip st in last ch-1 sp, ch 2; join with slip st to first slip st, finish off.

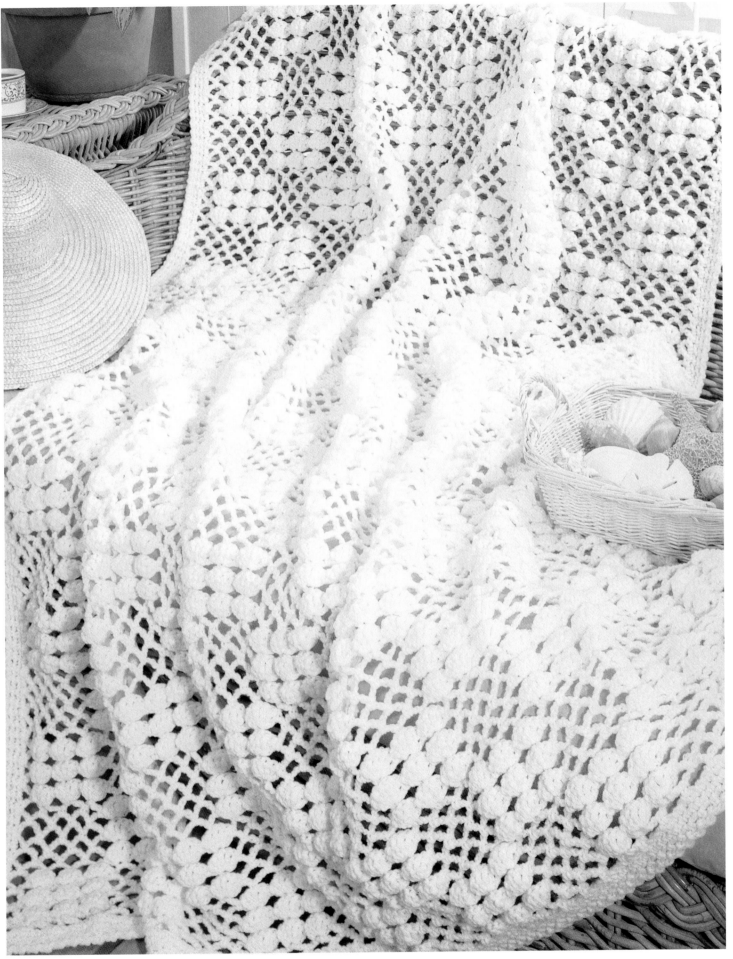

BUSY LIZZIES

Vibrant blooms, reminiscent of a path of vigorously flowering impatiens, enliven this floral afghan. Popcorns and clusters form the blossoms, which are worked in squares using a broad spectrum of colors.

Finished Size: 46" x 61"

MATERIALS
Worsted Weight Yarn:
  Dk Green - 23 ounces, (650 grams, 1,580 yards)
  Green - 13 ounces, (370 grams, 890 yards)
  Lt Green - 10 ounces, (280 grams, 685 yards)
  Pink - 1 ounce, (30 grams, 70 yards)
  Dk Pink - 1 ounce, (30 grams, 70 yards)
  Rose - 1 ounce, (30 grams, 70 yards)
  Lt Blue - 1 ounce, (30 grams, 70 yards)
  Blue - 1 ounce, (30 grams, 70 yards)
  Lt Purple - 1 ounce, (30 grams, 70 yards)
  Purple - 1 ounce, (30 grams, 70 yards)
  Dk Purple - 1 ounce, (30 grams, 70 yards)
Crochet hook, size I (5.50 mm) **or** size needed
  for gauge
Yarn needle

GAUGE SWATCH: Each Square = 5"

STITCH GUIDE

> **BEGINNING POPCORN**
> Ch 3, 3 dc in ring, drop loop from hook, insert hook in top of beginning ch-3, hook dropped loop and draw through *(Fig. 18a, page 136)*.
> **POPCORN**
> 4 Dc in ring, drop loop from hook, insert hook in first dc of 4-dc group, hook dropped loop and draw through.
> **BEGINNING CLUSTER**
> Ch 2, ★ YO, insert hook in sp indicated, YO and pull up a loop, YO and draw through 2 loops on hook; repeat from ★ once **more**, YO and draw through all 3 loops on hook *(Figs. 17a & b, page 136)*.
> **CLUSTER**
> ★ YO, insert hook in sp indicated, YO and pull up a loop, YO and draw through 2 loops on hook; repeat from ★ 2 times **more**, YO and draw through all 4 loops on hook.

SQUARE (Make 108)
Note: For Rnd 1, make 12 Squares **each** with Lt Pink, Pink, Dk Pink, Rose, Lt Blue, Blue, Lt Purple, Purple, and Dk Purple.

Rnd 1 (Right side): Work beginning Popcorn, ch 2, work Popcorn, ch 5, work (Popcorn, ch 2, Popcorn, ch 5) 3 times; join with slip st to top of beginning Popcorn, finish off: 4 ch-5 sps and 4 ch-2 sps.

Note: Loop a short piece of yarn around any stitch to mark Rnd 1 as **right** side.

Rnd 2: With **right** side facing, join Lt Green with slip st in any ch-5 sp; work (beginning Cluster, ch 3, Cluster) in same sp, ch 2, 3 dc in next ch-2 sp, ch 2, ★ work (Cluster, ch 3, Cluster) in next ch-5 sp, ch 2, 3 dc in next ch-2 sp, ch 2; repeat from ★ around; join with slip st to top of beginning Cluster, finish off: 12 sps.

Rnd 3: With **right** side facing, join Green with slip st in any ch-3 sp; work (beginning Cluster, ch 3, Cluster) in same sp, ch 2, 2 dc in next ch-2 sp, dc in next 3 dc, 2 dc in next ch-2 sp, ch 2, ★ work (Cluster, ch 3, Cluster) in next ch-3 sp, ch 2, 2 dc in next ch-2 sp, dc in next 3 dc, 2 dc in next ch-2 sp, ch 2; repeat from ★ around; join with slip st to top of beginning Cluster, finish off: 28 dc.

Rnd 4: With **right** side facing, join Dk Green with slip st in any ch-3 sp; work (beginning Cluster, ch 3, Cluster) in same sp, ch 2, 2 dc in next ch-2 sp, dc in next 7 dc, 2 dc in next ch-2 sp, ch 2, ★ work (Cluster, ch 3, Cluster) in next ch-3 sp, ch 2, 2 dc in next ch-2 sp, dc in next 7 dc, 2 dc in next ch-2 sp, ch 2; repeat from ★ around; join with slip st to top of beginning Cluster, finish off: 44 dc.

ASSEMBLY

With Dk Green, placing colors randomly, and working through inside loops only, whipstitch Squares together, forming 9 vertical strips of 12 Squares each *(Fig 35a, page 141)*, beginning in center ch of first corner and ending in center ch of next corner; whipstitch strips together in same manner.

EDGING

Rnd 1: With **right** side facing, join Dk Green with slip st in any dc; ch 1, sc evenly around working 3 sc in each corner ch-3 sp; join with slip st to first sc.

Rnd 2: Ch 1, sc in next st and in each sc around working 3 sc in center sc of each corner; join with slip st to first sc, finish off.

PRIMARY RAINBOW

*A rainbow of bright colors edged in black makes a bold statement
on this kid-friendly afghan. Worked holding two strands of yarn,
the extra-cozy cover-up is great for back-to-school time.*

Finished Size: 41" x 65"

MATERIALS
Worsted Weight Yarn:
Black - 25 ounces,
(710 grams, 1,415 yards)
Red - 5¹/₂ ounces,
(160 grams, 310 yards)
Blue - 5¹/₂ ounces,
(160 grams, 310 yards)
Orange - 5¹/₂ ounces,
(160 grams, 310 yards)
Green - 5¹/₂ ounces,
(160 grams, 310 yards)
Purple - 2¹/₂ ounces,
(70 grams, 140 yards)
Crochet hook, size Q (15.00 mm)
Yarn needle

Note: Entire Afghan is worked holding two
strands of yarn together.

GAUGE: Each Center = 3¹/₂" wide
9 sc = 5¹/₂"

STITCH GUIDE

LOOP
Ch 5, slip st in fifth ch from hook.

STRIP (Make 9)
CENTER
Make the number of Centers indicated with the following colors:
Red - 2, Blue - 2, Orange - 2, Green - 2, and Purple - 1.

Ch 101 **loosely**.
Row 1: Sc in second ch from hook and in each ch across:
100 sc.
Row 2 (Right side): Ch 3 **(counts as first dc)**, turn; dc in next
sc, ★ skip next sc, dc in next 3 sc, working **around** last 3 dc
made, dc in skipped sc; repeat from ★ across to last 2 sc, dc in
last 2 sc.
Note: Loop a short piece of yarn around first dc made to mark
bottom edge and to mark Row 2 as **right** side.
Row 3: Ch 1, turn; sc in each dc across; finish off.

BORDER
With **right** side facing, join Black with sc in first sc on Row 3
(see Joining With Sc, page 139); work Loop, (sc in next
2 sc, work Loop) across to last sc, sc in last sc; working in end
of rows, skip first row, 7 dc in next row, skip last row; working
in free loops of beginning ch **(Fig. 29b, page 139)**, sc in ch at
base of first sc, work Loop, (sc in next 2 chs, work Loop)
across to last ch, sc in last ch; working in end of rows, skip first
row, 7 dc in next row, skip last row; join with slip st to first sc,
finish off.

ASSEMBLY
Afghan is assembled by joining Strips in the following color
sequence: Red, Blue, Orange, Green, Purple, Green, Orange,
Blue, Red.

Join Strips as follows:
Place two Strips with **right** sides facing and bottom edges at the same end. Working from left to right, insert hook in first Loop at bottom of **right Strip**, pull first Loop at bottom of **left Strip** through Loop on hook, ★ pull next Loop on **right Strip** through Loop on hook, pull next Loop on **left Strip** through Loop on hook; repeat from ★ across; sew last Loop in place to **right Strip**.

Repeat for remaining Strips.

Braid Loops along outside edges of Afghan in same manner and sew in place.

GRANNY STRIPES

Put your scrap yarns to good use by making this striped granny afghan! Worked in strips, the wrap has a pretty patchwork effect.

Finished Size: 45" x 62"

MATERIALS
Worsted Weight Yarn:
Black - 24 ounces, (680 grams, 1,360 yards)
Scraps - 19 ounces, (540 grams, 1,075 yards) **total**
Crochet hook, size H (5.00 mm) **or** size needed
for gauge

GAUGE: Center = 2³/4" wide and 10 rows = 8"
Each Strip = 3¹/2" wide

Gauge Swatch: 3¹/2"w x 4³/4"h
Work same as Center for 5 rows.
Finish off.
Work Border.

FIRST STRIP
CENTER
With Black, ch 4; join with slip st to form a ring.
Row 1 (Right side): Ch 4 **(counts as first dc plus ch 1, now and throughout)**, (3 dc, ch 3, 3 dc, ch 1, dc) in ring.
Note: Loop a short piece of yarn around any stitch to mark bottom edge and to mark Row 1 as **right** side.
Row 2: Ch 4, turn; (3 dc, ch 3, 3 dc) in next ch-3 sp, ch 1, skip next 3 dc, dc in last dc changing to next color *(Fig. 31a, page 139)*.
Rows 3-11: Ch 4, turn; (3 dc, ch 3, 3 dc) in next ch-3 sp, ch 1, skip next 3 dc, dc in last dc.
Row 12: Ch 4, turn; (3 dc, ch 3, 3 dc) in next ch-3 sp, ch 1, skip next 3 dc, dc in last dc changing to Black.
Row 13: Ch 4, turn; (3 dc, ch 3, 3 dc) in next ch-3 sp, ch 1, skip next 3 dc, dc in last dc.
Row 14: Ch 4, turn; (3 dc, ch 3, 3 dc) in next ch-3 sp, ch 1, skip next 3 dc, dc in last dc changing to next color.
Rows 15-74: Repeat Rows 3-14, 5 times; do **not** change color at the end of Row 74.
Finish off.

BORDER
With **right** side facing, join Black with slip st in beginning ring; ch 3, (2 dc, ch 2, 3 dc) in same sp, ch 1; working in end of rows, skip first row, (3 dc, ch 2, 3 dc) in next row, ch 1, (3 dc in next row, ch 1) across to last row, (3 dc, ch 2, 3 dc) in last row, ch 1, (3 dc, ch 2, 3 dc) in next ch-3 sp, ch 1; working in end of rows, (3 dc, ch 2, 3 dc) in first row, ch 1, (3 dc in next row, ch 1) across to last 2 rows, (3 dc, ch 2, 3 dc) in next row, ch 1, skip last row; join with slip st to top of beginning ch-3, finish off.

REMAINING 12 STRIPS
CENTER
Work same as First Strip.

BORDER
Joining Rnd: With **right** side facing, join Black with slip st in beginning ring; ch 3, (2 dc, ch 2, 3 dc) in same sp, ch 1; working in end of rows, skip first row, (3 dc, ch 2, 3 dc) in next row, ch 1, (3 dc in next row, ch 1) across to last row, (3 dc, ch 2, 3 dc) in last row, ch 1, (3 dc, ch 2, 3 dc) in next ch-3 sp, ch 1; working in end of rows, 3 dc in first row, ch 1, holding Strips with **wrong** sides together and bottom edges at the same end, slip st in corresponding ch-2 sp on **previous Strip** *(Fig. 32, page 140)*, ch 1, 3 dc in same row on **new Strip**, ch 1, slip st in next ch-1 sp on **previous Strip**, ★ 3 dc in next row on **new Strip**, ch 1, slip st in next ch-1 sp on **previous Strip**; repeat from ★ across to last 2 rows on **new Strip**, 3 dc in next row on **new Strip**, ch 1, slip st in next ch-2 sp on **previous Strip**, ch 1, 3 dc in same row on **new Strip**, ch 1, skip last row; join with slip st to top of beginning ch-3, finish off.

BROWN-EYED SUSANS

*The flowers on this country throw don't need watering —
they're guaranteed to bloom for years! Masses of brown-eyed
Susans make this afghan a gardener's delight.*

Finished Size: 48" x 66"

MATERIALS
Worsted Weight Yarn:
   Yellow - 26 ounces, (740 grams, 1,785 yards)
   Brown - 4 ounces, (110 grams, 275 yards)
   Green - 15 ounces, (430 grams, 1,030 yards)
Crochet hook, size I (5.50 mm) **or** size needed
   for gauge

GAUGE: Each Flower (across Short Petals) = 2³/₄"
   Each Strip = 5¹/₄" wide

STITCH GUIDE

DECREASE
Pull up a loop in next 2 sc, YO and draw through all 3 loops on hook **(counts as one sc)**.

FIRST STRIP
CENTER
FIRST FLOWER
With Brown, ch 4; join with slip st to form a ring.
Rnd 1 (Right side)**:** Ch 1, 8 sc in ring; join with slip st to first sc, finish off: 8 sc.
Note: Loop a short piece of yarn around any stitch to mark Rnd 1 as **right** side.
Rnd 2: With **right** side facing, join Yellow with slip st in any sc; ch 1, sc in same st, ★ † ch 6, sc in second ch from hook, hdc in next 4 chs, sc in next sc on Rnd 1 **(Long Petal made)**, ch 4, sc in second ch from hook, hdc in next 2 chs †, sc in next sc on Rnd 1 **(Short Petal made)**; repeat from ★ 2 times **more**, then repeat from † to † once; join with slip st to first sc, finish off: 8 Petals.
NEXT 22 FLOWERS
With Brown, ch 4; join with slip st to form a ring.
Rnd 1 (Right side)**:** Ch 1, 8 sc in ring; join with slip st to first sc, finish off: 8 sc.
Note: Mark Rnd 1 as **right** side.

Rnd 2 (Joining rnd)**:** With **right** side facing, join Yellow with slip st in any sc; ch 1, sc in same st, ch 6, sc in second ch from hook, hdc in next 4 chs, sc in next sc on Rnd 1, ★ ch 4, sc in second ch from hook, hdc in next 2 chs, sc in next sc on Rnd 1, ch 6, sc in second ch from hook, hdc in next 4 chs, sc in next sc; repeat from ★ 2 times **more**, ch 3; holding Flowers with **wrong** sides together and matching Petals, slip st in end of Short Petal on **previous Flower** *(Fig. 32, page 140)*, sc in next ch on **new Flower**, hdc in next 2 chs; join with slip st to first sc, finish off: 8 Petals.

BORDER
Rnd 1: With **right** side facing and holding Strip with First Flower at top, join Green with slip st in end of second Long Petal to right of joining on First Flower; ch 1, sc in same st, ch 4, (sc in end of next Petal, ch 4) 3 times, † sc in end of next Petal on same Flower and on next Flower, ch 4, ★ sc in end of next Petal, ch 4, sc in end of next Petal on same Flower and on next Flower, ch 4; repeat from ★ 20 times **more** †, (sc in end of next Petal, ch 4) 5 times, repeat from † to † once, sc in end of last Petal, ch 4; join with slip st to first sc: 140 sc and 96 ch-4 sps.
Rnd 2: Ch 1, sc in same st, ch 1, [(tr, ch 1) 4 times in next ch-4 sp, sc in next sc, ch 1] 3 times, † (tr, ch 1) 3 times in next ch-4 sp, decrease, ch 1, (tr, ch 1) 3 times in next ch-4 sp, sc in next sc, ch 1 †, repeat from † to † 21 times **more**, [(tr, ch 1) 4 times in next ch-4 sp, sc in next sc, ch 1] 4 times, repeat from † to † 22 times, (tr, ch 1) 4 times in last ch-4 sp; join with slip st to first sc, finish off: 392 ch-1 sps.
Rnd 3: With **right** side facing, join Yellow with slip st in first ch-1 sp to left of joining; ch 1, sc in same sp, ★ † (ch 2, sc in next ch-1 sp) across to next sc, skip next sc †, sc in next ch-1 sp; repeat from ★ around to last 4 ch-1 sps, then repeat from † to † once; join with slip st to first sc: 296 ch-2 sps.
Rnd 4: Slip st in first ch-2 sp, ch 1, sc in same sp, [(ch 2, sc in next ch-2 sp) 3 times, ch 1, skip next sc, slip st in next sc, sc in next ch-2 sp] 3 times, † (ch 2, sc in next ch-2 sp) twice, ch 1, skip next sc, slip st in next sc, sc in next ch-2 sp †, repeat from † to † 43 times **more**, [(ch 2, sc in next ch-2 sp) 3 times, ch 1, skip next sc, slip st in next sc, sc in next ch-2 sp] 4 times, repeat from † to † 44 times, (ch 2, sc in next ch-2 sp) 3 times, ch 1, skip next sc, slip st in next sc; join with slip st to first sc, finish off.

REMAINING 8 STRIPS

Work same as First Strip through Rnd 3 of Border: 296 ch-2 sps.

Rnd 4 (Joining rnd)**:** Slip st in first ch-2 sp, ch 1, sc in same sp, [(ch 2, sc in next ch-2 sp) 3 times, ch 1, skip next sc, slip st in next sc, sc in next ch-2 sp] 3 times, ★ (ch 2, sc in next ch-2 sp) twice, ch 1, skip next sc, slip st in next sc, sc in next ch-2 sp; repeat from ★ 43 times **more**, [(ch 2, sc in next ch-2 sp) 3 times, ch 1, skip next sc, slip st in next sc, sc in next ch-2 sp] 3 times, ch 2, sc in next ch-2 sp, ch 1; holding Strips with **wrong** sides together and bottom edges at same end, [slip st in corresponding ch-2 sp on **previous Strip** *(Fig. 32, page 140)*, ch 1, sc in next ch-2 sp on **new** Strip, ch 1] twice, skip next sc, slip st in next sc, sc in next ch-2 sp, (ch 1, slip st in next ch-2 sp on **previous Strip**, ch 1, sc in next ch-2 sp on **new Strip**) twice, † ch 1, skip next sc, slip st in next sc, sc in next ch-2 sp, (ch 1, slip st in next ch-2 sp on **previous Strip**, ch 1, sc in next ch-2 sp on **new Strip**) twice †, repeat from † to † 43 times **more**, ch 2, sc in next ch-2 sp, ch 1, skip next sc, slip st in next sc; join with slip st to first sc, finish off.

BANDANNA BLOCKS

Resembling the spokes of a wheel, the motifs in this handsome throw recall the covered wagons of the Old West. The bandanna-inspired afghan is great for snuggling on fall hayrides.

Finished Size: 49" x 66"

MATERIALS

Worsted Weight Yarn:
  Blue - 40 ounces, (1,140 grams, 2,630 yards)
  White - 10 ounces, (280 grams, 655 yards)
  Black - 10 ounces, (280 grams, 655 yards)
Crochet hook, size I (5.50 mm) **or** size needed
  for gauge
Yarn needle

GAUGE: Each Square = 8¹/₂"

Gauge Swatch: 4"
Work same as Square Rnds 1-4.

STITCH GUIDE

> **DOUBLE TREBLE CROCHET**
> *(abbreviated dtr)*
> YO 3 times, insert hook in st indicated, YO and pull up a loop,
> (YO and draw through 2 loops on hook) 4 times
> *(Figs. 8a & b, page 134)*.

SQUARE (Make 35)

Rnd 1 (Right side)**:** With Blue, ch 5, (dc, ch 1) 7 times in fifth ch from hook; join with slip st to fourth ch of beginning ch-5, finish off: 8 ch-1 sps.

Note: Loop a short piece of yarn around any stitch to mark Rnd 1 as **right** side.

Rnd 2: With **right** side facing, join White with slip st in any ch-1 sp; ch 3 **(counts as first dc, now and throughout)**, 2 dc in same sp, ch 1, (3 dc in next ch-1 sp, ch 1) around; join with slip st to first dc, finish off: 24 dc.

Rnd 3: With **right** side facing, join Blue with sc in first dc of any 3-dc group **(see Joining With Sc, page 139)**; sc in next 2 dc, working in **front** of next ch-1, tr in st one rnd **below** ch-1, ★ sc in next 3 dc, working in **front** of next ch-1, tr in st one rnd **below** ch-1; repeat from ★ around; join with slip st to first sc, finish off: 32 sts.

Rnd 4: With **right** side facing, join Black with slip st in any tr; ch 2 **(counts as first hdc)**, hdc in next sc, 2 hdc in next sc, (hdc in next 3 sts, 2 hdc in next sc) around to last sc, hdc in last sc; join with slip st to first hdc, finish off: 40 hdc.

Rnd 5: With **right** side facing, join Blue with slip st in same st as joining; ch 3, tr in same st, ★ † ch 1, dtr in next hdc, ch 1, (tr, dc) in next hdc, hdc in next 2 hdc, sc in next 3 hdc, hdc in next 2 hdc †, (dc, tr) in next hdc; repeat from ★ 2 times **more**, then repeat from † to † once; join with slip st to first dc, finish off: 48 sts and 8 ch-1 sps.

Rnd 6: With **wrong** side facing, join White with sc in first ch to **left** of any corner dtr; ★ † ch 1, skip next tr, (sc in next st, ch 1, skip next st) across to first ch of next corner, sc in ch, ch 3, skip next dtr †, sc in next ch; repeat from ★ 2 times **more**, then repeat from † to † once; join with slip st to first sc, finish off: 28 sc and 28 sps.

Rnd 7: With **right** side facing, join Blue with sc in first sc to **left** of any corner ch-3 sp; ★ † (working **behind** next ch-1, dc in st one rnd **below** ch-1, sc in next sc) 6 times, working in **front** of next ch-3, (dc, ch 1, tr, ch 1, dc) in dtr one rnd **below** ch-3 †, sc in next sc; repeat from ★ 2 times **more**, then repeat from † to † once; join with slip st to first sc, finish off: 64 sts and 8 ch-1 sps.

Rnd 8: With **wrong** side facing, join Black with sc in first ch to **left** of any corner tr; ★ † ch 1, skip next dc, (sc in next sc, ch 1, skip next dc) across to first ch of next corner, sc in ch, ch 3, skip next tr †, sc in next ch; repeat from ★ 2 times **more**, then repeat from † to † once; join with slip st to first sc, finish off: 36 sc and 36 sps.

Rnd 9: With **right** side facing, join Blue with sc in first sc to **left** of any corner ch-3 sp; ★ † working **behind** next ch-1, dc in dc one rnd **below** ch-1, sc in next sc, working in **front** of next ch-1, dc in dc one rnd **below** ch-1, sc in next sc, (working **behind** next ch-1, dc in dc one rnd **below** ch-1, sc in next sc) 4 times, working in **front** of next ch-1, dc in dc one rnd **below** ch-1, sc in next sc, working **behind** next ch-1, dc in dc one rnd **below** ch-1, sc in next sc, working **behind** next ch-3, (dc, ch 1, tr, ch 1, dc) in tr one rnd **below** ch-3 †, sc in next sc; repeat from ★ 2 times **more**, then repeat from † to † once; join with slip st to first sc, finish off: 80 sts and 8 ch-1 sps.

Continued on page 100.

Rnd 10: With White, repeat Rnd 8: 44 sc and 44 sps.

Rnd 11: With **right** side facing, join Blue with sc in first sc to **left** of any corner ch-3 sp; ★ † working **behind** next ch-1, dc in dc one rnd **below** ch-1, sc in next sc, working in **front** of next ch-1, dc in dc one rnd **below** ch-1, sc in next sc, (working **behind** next ch-1, dc in dc one rnd **below** ch-1, sc in next sc) 6 times, working in **front** of next ch-1, dc in dc one rnd **below** ch-1, sc in next sc, working **behind** next ch-1, dc in dc one rnd **below** ch-1, sc in next sc, working **behind** next ch-3, (dc, ch 1, tr, ch 1, dc) in tr one rnd **below** ch-3 †, sc in next sc; repeat from ★ 2 times **more**, then repeat from † to † once; join with slip st to first sc, finish off: 96 sts and 8 ch-1 sps.

Rnd 12: Repeat Rnd 8: 52 sc and 52 sps.

Rnd 13: With **right** side facing, join Blue with sc in first sc to **left** of any corner ch-3 sp; ★ † working **behind** next ch-1, dc in dc one rnd **below** ch-1, sc in next sc, (working in **front** of next ch-1, dc in dc one rnd **below** ch-1, sc in next sc) 10 times, working **behind** next ch-1, dc in dc one rnd **below** ch-1, sc in next sc, working **behind** next ch-3, (dc, ch 3, dc) in tr one rnd **below** ch-3 †, sc in next sc; repeat from ★ 2 times **more**, then repeat from † to † once; join with slip st to first sc, finish off: 108 sts and 4 ch-3 sps.

ASSEMBLY

Using Blue and working through both loops, whipstitch Squares together, forming 5 vertical strips of 7 Squares each *(Fig. 35b, page 141)*, beginning in center ch of first corner and ending in center ch of next corner; whipstitch strips together in same manner.

BORDER

Rnd 1: With **right** side facing, join Blue with sc in any corner ch-3 sp; ch 2, sc in same sp and in next 27 sts, (sc in next sp, hdc in joining, sc in next sp and in next 27 sts) across to next corner ch-3 sp, ★ (sc, ch 2, sc) in corner ch-3 sp, sc in next 27 sts, (sc in next sp, hdc in joining, sc in next sp and in next 27 sts) across to next corner ch-3 sp; repeat from ★ 2 times **more**; join with slip st to first sc, finish off: 716 sc and 4 ch-2 sps.

Rnd 2: With **wrong** side facing, join White with sc in first sc to **left** of any corner ch-2 sp; ★ † (ch 1, skip next sc, sc in next sc) across to next corner ch-2 sp, ch 3, skip corner ch-2 sp †, sc in next sc; repeat from ★ 2 times **more**, then repeat from † to † once; join with slip st to first sc, finish off: 360 sc and 360 sps.

Rnd 3: With **right** side facing, join Blue with sc in first sc to **left** of any corner ch-3 sp; ★ † working **behind** next ch-1, dc in sc one rnd **below** ch-1, sc in next sc, (working in **front** of next ch-1, dc in sc one rnd **below** ch-1, sc in next sc) 3 times, (working **behind** next ch-1, dc in sc one rnd **below** ch-1, sc in next sc) 6 times, [(working in **front** of next ch-1, dc in sc one rnd **below** ch-1, sc in next sc) twice, (working **behind** next ch-1, dc in st one rnd **below** ch-1, sc in next sc) 5 times, (working in **front** of next ch-1, dc in sc one rnd **below** ch-1, sc in next sc) twice, (working **behind** next ch-1, dc in sc one rnd **below** ch-1, sc in next sc) 6 times] across to within 4 ch-1 sps of next corner ch-3 sp, (working in **front** of next ch-1, dc in sc one rnd **below** ch-1, sc in next sc) 3 times, working **behind** next ch-1, dc in sc one rnd **below** ch-1, sc in next sc, working **behind** corner ch-3, (dc, ch 1, tr, ch 1, dc) in ch-2 sp one rnd **below** ch-3 †, sc in next sc; repeat from ★ 2 times **more**, then repeat from † to † once; join with slip st to first sc, finish off: 728 sts and 8 ch-1 sps.

Rnd 4: With **wrong** side facing, join Black with sc in first ch to **left** of any corner tr; ★ † ch 1, skip next dc, (sc in next sc, ch 1, skip next dc) across to first ch of next corner, sc in ch, ch 3, skip next tr †, sc in next ch; repeat from ★ 2 times **more**, then repeat from † to † once; join with slip st to first sc, finish off: 368 sc and 368 sps.

Rnd 5: With **right** side facing, join Blue with sc in first sc to **left** of any corner ch-3 sp; ★ † working **behind** next ch-1, dc in dc one rnd **below** ch-1, sc in next sc, (working in **front** of next ch-1, dc in dc one rnd **below** ch-1, sc in next sc) 5 times, (working **behind** next ch-1, dc in dc one rnd **below** ch-1, sc in next sc) 4 times, [(working in **front** of next ch-1, dc in dc one rnd **below** ch-1, sc in next sc) 4 times, (working **behind** next ch-1, dc in dc one rnd **below** ch-1, sc in next sc) 3 times, (working in **front** of next ch-1, dc in dc one rnd **below** ch-1, sc in next sc) 4 times, (working **behind** next ch-1, dc in dc one rnd **below** ch-1, sc in next sc) 4 times] across to within 6 ch-1 sps of next corner ch-3 sp, (working in **front** of next ch-1, dc in dc one rnd **below** ch-1, sc in next sc) 5 times, working **behind** next ch-1, dc in dc one rnd **below** ch-1, sc in next sc, working **behind** corner ch-3, (dc, ch 1, tr, ch 1, dc) in tr one rnd **below** ch-3 †, sc in next sc; repeat from ★ 2 times **more**, then repeat from † to † once; join with slip st to first sc, finish off: 744 sts and 8 ch-1 sps.

Rnd 6: With White, repeat Rnd 4: 376 sc and 376 sps.

Rnd 7: With **right** side facing, join Blue with sc in first sc to **left** of any corner ch-3 sp; ★ † working **behind** next ch-1, dc in dc one rnd **below** ch-1, sc in next sc, (working in **front** of next ch-1, dc in dc one rnd **below** ch-1, sc in next sc) 7 times, (working **behind** next ch-1, dc in dc one rnd **below** ch-1, sc in next sc) twice, [(working in **front** of next ch-1, dc in dc one rnd **below** ch-1, sc in next sc) 6 times, working **behind** next ch-1, dc in dc one rnd **below** ch-1, sc in next sc, (working in **front** of next ch-1, dc in dc one rnd **below** ch-1, sc in next sc) 6 times, (working **behind** next ch-1, dc in dc one rnd **below** ch-1, sc in next sc) twice] across to within 8 ch-1 sps of next corner ch-3 sp, (working in **front** of next ch-1, dc in dc one rnd **below** ch-1, sc in next sc) 7 times, working **behind** next ch-1, dc in dc one rnd **below** ch-1, sc in next sc, working **behind** corner ch-3, (dc, ch 1, tr, ch 1, dc) in tr one rnd **below** ch-3 †, sc in next sc; repeat from ★ 2 times **more**, then repeat from † to † once; join with slip st to first sc, finish off: 760 sts and 8 ch-1 sps.

Rnd 8: Repeat Rnd 4: 384 sc and 384 sps.

Rnd 9: With **right** side facing, join Blue with sc in first sc to **left** of any corner ch-3 sp; ★ † working **behind** next ch-1, dc in dc one rnd **below** ch-1, sc in next sc, (working in **front** of next ch-1, dc in dc one rnd **below** ch-1, sc in next sc) 7 times, (working **behind** next ch-1, dc in dc one rnd **below** ch-1, sc in next sc) 4 times, [(working in **front** of next ch-1, dc in dc one rnd **below** ch-1, sc in next sc) 4 times, (working **behind** next ch-1, dc in dc one rnd **below** ch-1, sc in next sc) 3 times, (working in **front** of next ch-1, dc in dc one rnd **below** ch-1, sc in next sc) 4 times, (working **behind** next ch-1, dc in dc one rnd **below** ch-1, sc in next sc) 4 times] across to within 8 ch-1 sps of next corner ch-3 sp, (working in **front** of next ch-1, dc in dc one rnd **below** ch-1, sc in next sc) 7 times, working **behind** next ch-1, dc in dc one rnd **below** ch-1, sc in next sc, working **behind** corner ch-3, (dc, ch 1, tr, ch 1, dc) in tr one rnd **below** ch-3 †, sc in next sc; repeat from ★ 2 times **more**, then repeat from † to † once; join with slip st to first sc, finish off: 776 sts and 8 ch-1 sps.

Rnd 10: With White, repeat Rnd 4: 392 sc and 392 sps.

Rnd 11: With **right** side facing, join Blue with sc in first sc to **left** of any corner ch-3 sp; ★ † working **behind** next ch-1, dc in dc one rnd **below** ch-1, sc in next sc, (working in **front** of next ch-1, dc in dc one rnd **below** ch-1, sc in next sc) 7 times, (working **behind** next ch-1, dc in dc one rnd **below** ch-1, sc in next sc) 6 times, [(working in **front** of next ch-1, dc in dc one rnd **below** ch-1, sc in next sc) twice, (working **behind** next ch-1, dc in dc one rnd **below** ch-1, sc in next sc) 5 times, (working in **front** of next ch-1, dc in dc one rnd **below** ch-1, sc in next sc) twice, (working **behind** next ch-1, dc in dc one rnd **below** ch-1, sc in next sc) 6 times] across to within 8 ch-1 sps of next corner ch-3 sp, (working in **front** of next ch-1, dc in dc one rnd **below** ch-1, sc in next sc) 7 times, working **behind** next ch-1, dc in dc one rnd **below** ch-1, sc in next sc, working **behind** corner ch-3, (dc, ch 1, tr, ch 1, dc) in tr one rnd **below** ch-3 †, sc in next sc; repeat from ★ 2 times **more**, then repeat from † to † once; join with slip st to first sc, do **not** finish off: 792 sts and 8 ch-1 sps.

Rnd 12: Ch 2, skip next dc, ★ (slip st in next sc, ch 2, skip next dc) across to first ch-1 sp of next corner, slip st in ch-1 sp, ch 3, skip next tr, slip st in next ch-1 sp, ch 2, skip next dc; repeat from ★ around; join with slip st to first slip st, finish off.

RADIANT MUMS

Blooming in masses everywhere you turn, chrysanthemums have become an American symbol of autumn. This sunny spread radiates with the beauty of these magnificent flowers.

Finished Size: 46" x 68"

MATERIALS

Worsted Weight Yarn:

Off-White - 32 ounces,
(910 grams, 1,865 yards)

Gold - 2½ ounces,
(70 grams, 145 yards)

Lt Orange - 5 ounces,
(140 grams, 290 yards)

Orange - 11 ounces,
(310 grams, 640 yards)

Green - 8 ounces,
(230 grams, 465 yards)

Crochet hook, size G (4.00 mm) **or** size needed for gauge

Yarn needle

GAUGE: Each Square = 7½"

Gauge Swatch: 4"
Work same as Square Rnds 1-3.

STITCH GUIDE

BEGINNING CLUSTER

Ch 2, ★ YO, insert hook in st or sp indicated, YO and pull up a loop, YO and draw through 2 loops on hook; repeat from ★ once **more**, YO and draw through all 3 loops on hook *(Figs. 17a & b, page 136)*.

CLUSTER

★ YO, insert hook in st or sp indicated, YO and pull up a loop, YO and draw through 2 loops on hook; repeat from ★ 2 times **more**, YO and draw through all 4 loops on hook.

SQUARE (Make 54)

With Gold, ch 4; join with slip st to form a ring.

Rnd 1 (Right side)**:** Ch 3 **(counts as first dc, now and throughout)**, 11 dc in ring; join with slip st to first dc, finish off: 12 dc.

Note: Loop a short piece of yarn around any stitch to mark Rnd 1 as **right** side.

Rnd 2: With **right** side facing, join Lt Orange with slip st in any dc; work beginning Cluster in same st, ch 1, (work Cluster in next dc, ch 1) around; join with slip st to top of beginning Cluster, finish off: 12 Clusters and 12 ch-1 sps.

Rnd 3: With **right** side facing, join Orange with slip st in any ch-1 sp; work beginning Cluster in same sp, ch 1, work Cluster in next Cluster, ch 1, ★ work Cluster in next ch-1 sp, ch 1, work Cluster in next Cluster, ch 1; repeat from ★ around; join with slip st to top of beginning Cluster, finish off: 24 Clusters and 24 ch-1 sps.

Rnd 4: With **right** side facing, join Green with slip st in any ch-1 sp; ch 3, (dc, tr, ch 2, tr, 2 dc) in same sp, ch 1, (sc in next ch-1 sp, ch 1) 5 times, ★ (2 dc, tr, ch 2, tr, 2 dc) in next ch-1 sp, ch 1, (sc in next ch-1 sp, ch 1) 5 times; repeat from ★ around; join with slip st to first dc, finish off: 28 sps.

Rnd 5: With **right** side facing, join Off-White with slip st in any ch-2 sp; ch 3, (dc, ch 2, 2 dc) in same sp, dc in next 3 sts, 2 in each of next 6 ch-1 sps, dc in next 3 sts, ★ (2 dc, ch 2, 2 dc) in next ch-2 sp, dc in next 3 sts, 2 dc in each of next 6 ch-1 sps, dc in next 3 sts; repeat from ★ around; join with slip st to first dc, do **not** finish off: 88 dc.

Continued on page 110.

BLUE RIBBON WINNER

This winning throw will surely earn a blue ribbon at the county fair!
It features dynamic diamonds accented with pretty popcorn "flowers."
A flowing fringe gives the prized wrap a fanciful finish.

Finished Size: 51" x 71"

MATERIALS

Worsted Weight Yarn:
  White - 16 ounces, (450 grams, 1,050 yards)
  Lt Blue - 11½ ounces, (330 grams, 755 yards)
  Blue - 13½ ounces, (380 grams, 885 yards)
  Dk Blue - 21½ ounces, (610 grams, 1,415 yards)
Crochet hook, size I (5.50 mm) **or** size needed
  for gauge
Yarn needle

GAUGE: Each Square = 10"

Gauge Swatch: 5"
Work same as Center.

STITCH GUIDE

> **BEGINNING POPCORN**
> Ch 3, 3 dc in sp indicated, drop loop from hook, insert hook in top of beginning ch-3, hook dropped loop and draw through *(Fig. 18a, page 136)*.
> **POPCORN**
> 4 Dc in st or sp indicated, drop loop from hook, insert hook in first dc of 4-dc group, hook dropped loop and draw through.

SQUARE (Make 35)

CENTER

With White, ch 4; join with slip st to form a ring.
Rnd 1 (Right side): Work beginning Popcorn in ring, ch 3, (work Popcorn in ring, ch 3) 3 times; join with slip st to top of beginning Popcorn, finish off: 4 Popcorns.
Note: Loop a short piece of yarn around any stitch to mark Rnd 1 as **right** side.
Rnd 2: With **right** side facing, join Lt Blue with slip st in any ch-3 sp; ch 3 **(counts as first dc, now and throughout)**, (2 dc, ch 2, 3 dc) in same sp, ch 1, ★ (3 dc, ch 2, 3 dc) in next ch-3 sp, ch 1; repeat from ★ around; join with slip st to first dc, finish off: 8 sps.

Rnd 3: With **right** side facing, join Blue with slip st in any ch-2 sp; work (beginning Popcorn, ch 3, Popcorn) in same sp (corner made), ch 3, work Popcorn in next ch-1 sp, ch 3, ★ work (Popcorn, ch 3, Popcorn) in next ch-2 sp (corner made), ch 3, work Popcorn in next ch-1 sp, ch 3; repeat from ★ around; join with slip st to top of beginning Popcorn, finish off: 12 ch-3 sps.
Rnd 4: With **right** side facing, join Dk Blue with slip st in any corner ch-3 sp; ch 3, (2 dc, ch 2, 3 dc) in same sp, ch 1, (3 dc in next ch-3 sp, ch 1) twice, ★ (3 dc, ch 2, 3 dc) in next corner ch-3 sp, ch 1, (3 dc in next ch-3 sp, ch 1) twice; repeat from ★ around; join with slip st to first dc, finish off: 48 dc and 16 sps.

CORNER TRIANGLES

FIRST TRIANGLE

Row 1: With **right** side facing and working in Back Loops Only *(Fig. 28, page 139)*, join White with slip st in second ch of any corner ch-2 sp; ch 1, sc in same st and in each dc and each ch across to next corner ch-2 sp, sc in next ch: 17 sc.
Rows 2-8: Ch 1, turn; working in both loops, skip first sc, sc in each sc across to last 2 sc, skip next sc, sc in last sc: 3 sc.
Row 9: Ch 1, turn; skip first sc, pull up a loop in last 2 sc, YO and draw through all 3 loops on hook; finish off.

REMAINING 3 TRIANGLES

Row 1: With **right** side facing and working in Back Loops Only, join White with slip st in next ch on Rnd 4 of Center to **left** of last Corner Triangle; ch 1, sc in same st and in each dc and each ch across to next corner ch-2 sp, sc in next ch: 17 sc.
Rows 2-9: Work same as First Triangle; at end of fourth Triangle do **not** finish off.

BORDER

Rnd 1: Ch 1, ★ work 9 sc evenly spaced across end of rows on same Triangle, sc in same st as last sc on Row 1 of same Triangle and in same st as first sc on Row 1 of next Triangle, work 9 sc evenly spaced across end of rows on same Triangle, ch 2; repeat from ★ around; join with slip st to first sc, finish off: 80 sc and 4 ch-2 sps.

Continued on page 111.

105

BOW TIES

Long double crochets form fanciful "bow ties" along the strips of this casual throw. The double-strand mile-a-minute creation looks cozy worked in soft green and ecru.

Finished Size: 51" x 66"

MATERIALS

Worsted Weight Yarn:
  Ecru - 48 ounces, (1,360 grams, 3,155 yards)
  Green - 46 ounces, (1,310 grams, 3,025 yards)
Crochet hook, size K (6.50 mm) **or** size needed
  for gauge
Yarn needle

Note: Entire Afghan is worked holding two strands of yarn
  together.

GAUGE: Each Strip = 5$\frac{1}{2}$"

Gauge Swatch: 3"w x 7$\frac{1}{2}$"h
Ch 13 **loosely**.
Work same as Center.
Work Border Rnds 1-2.
Finish off.

STITCH GUIDE

LONG DOUBLE CROCHET
  (abbreviated LDC)
YO, insert hook in sp indicated, YO and pull up a loop even
with last st made, (YO and draw through 2 loops on hook)
twice *(Fig. 20, page 137)*.

DECREASE
Pull up a loop in next dc on **same Strip**, skip joining, pull
up a loop in next dc on **next Strip**, YO and draw through
all 3 loops on hook.

REVERSE SINGLE CROCHET
Working from **left** to **right**, ★ insert hook in st to right of
hook, YO and draw through, under, and to left of loop on
hook (2 loops on hook), YO and draw through both loops
on hook **(reverse sc made)**; repeat from ★ around
(Figs. 27a-d, page 138).

STRIP (Make 9)
CENTER
With Ecru, ch 160 **loosely**.

Row 1 (Right side)**:** Sc in second ch from hook and in each ch
across: 159 sc.

Note: Loop a short piece of yarn around first stitch made to
mark bottom edge and to mark Row 1 as **right** side.

Row 2: Ch 4 **(counts as first dc plus ch 1)**, turn; skip next
sc, dc in next 2 sc, ch 1, place marker around last ch-1 made
for joining placement, ★ skip next sc, dc in next 2 sc, ch 1;
repeat from ★ across to last 2 sc, skip next sc, dc in last sc:
106 dc and 53 ch-1 sps.

Row 3: Ch 1, turn; sc in each dc and in each ch-1 sp across;
finish off.

BORDER

Rnd 1: With **right** side facing, working around Row 3 and in
ch-1 sps on Row 2 of Center, join Green with slip st in marked
ch-1 sp, remove marker; ch 3 **(counts as first LDC)**, work
LDC in same sp, work 15 LDC in last ch-1 sp; working around
Row 1 and in ch-1 sps on Row 2 of Center, work 3 LDC in each
ch-1 sp across to last ch-1 sp, work 15 LDC in last ch-1 sp;
working over Row 3 and in ch-1 sps on Row 2 of Center, work
3 LDC in each ch-1 sp across, work LDC in same sp as first LDC;
join with slip st to first LDC, finish off: 336 LDC.

Rnd 2: With **right** side facing, join Ecru with sc in second LDC
of either 15-LDC group **(see Joining With Sc, page 139)**; sc
in next 3 LDC, † 2 sc in next LDC, (sc in next LDC, 2 sc in next
LDC) twice, sc in next 4 LDC, skip next dc on Row 2 of Center,
work 2 LDC in sp **before** next dc **(Fig. 33, page 140)**, ★ sc
in center LDC of next 3-LDC group, skip next 2 dc on Row 2 of
Center from last LDC made, work 2 LDC in sp **before** next dc;
repeat from ★ across to next 15-LDC group †, sc in second LDC
of 15-LDC group and in next 3 LDC, repeat from † to † once;
join with slip st to first sc: 342 sts.

Continued on page 111.

FOREST DREAM

Crocheted in shades of green, this textured throw will have you dreaming of a tranquil forest glade. Long double crochets, set against a background of single crochets, create the distinctive pattern of "pinecones."

Finished Size: 52" x 67"

MATERIALS

Worsted Weight Yarn:
   Dk Green - 20 ounces, (570 grams, 1,315 yards)
   Green - 30 ounces, (850 grams, 1,970 yards)
   Lt Green - 7¹/₂ ounces, (210 grams, 495 yards)
Crochet hook, size G (4.00 mm) **or** size needed
   for gauge

GAUGE: 14 sts and 14 rows = 4"

Note: Each row is worked across the length of Afghan. All rows are worked in Back Loops Only *(Fig. 28, page 139)* and with **right** side facing throughout. When joining yarn and finishing off, leave a 5" length to be worked into fringe.

STITCH GUIDE

> **LONG DOUBLE CROCHET**
> *(abbreviated LDC)*
> YO, working around previous 2 rows, insert hook in Back Loop Only of st 2 rows **below** next sc, YO and pull up a loop even with loop on hook *(Fig. 20, page 137)*, (YO and draw through 2 loops on hook) twice.
>
> **SPLIT LONG DOUBLE CROCHET**
> *(abbreviated Split LDC)*
> YO, working around previous row, insert hook through post of LDC one row **below** next sc *(Fig. 21, page 137)*, YO and pull up a loop even with loop on hook, (YO and draw through 2 loops on hook) twice.

COLOR SEQUENCE

3 Rows Dk Green, ★ 2 rows Green, one row Lt Green, 2 rows Green, 2 rows Dk Green, 2 rows Green, one row Lt Green, 2 rows Green, 3 rows Dk Green; repeat from ★ 11 times **more**.

With Dk Green, ch 234 **loosely**.

Row 1 (Right side): Sc in back ridge of second ch from hook *(Fig. 2b, page 133)* and in each ch across; finish off: 233 sc.

Note: Loop a short piece of yarn around any stitch to mark Row 1 as **right** side.

Rows 2 and 3: Join Dk Green with sc in first sc *(see Joining With Sc, page 139)*; sc in each sc across; finish off.

Row 4: Join next color with sc in first sc; sc in next 5 sts, work LDC, ★ sc in next 21 sts, work LDC; repeat from ★ across to last 6 sts, sc in last 6 sts; finish off: 11 LDC and 222 sc.

Row 5: Join next color with sc in first sc; sc in next 4 sts, work LDC, sc in next st, work LDC, ★ sc in next 19 sts, work LDC, sc in next st, work LDC; repeat from ★ across to last 5 sts, sc in last 5 sts; finish off: 22 LDC and 211 sc.

Row 6: Join next color with sc in first sc; (sc in next 3 sts, work LDC) twice, ★ sc in next 17 sts, work LDC, sc in next 3 sts, work LDC; repeat from ★ across to last 4 sts, sc in last 4 sts; finish off.

Row 7: Join next color with sc in first sc; (sc in next 2 sts, work LDC) 3 times, ★ sc in next 15 sts, work LDC, (sc in next 2 sts, work LDC) twice; repeat from ★ across to last 3 sts, sc in last 3 sts; finish off: 33 LDC and 200 sc.

Row 8: Join next color with sc in first sc; sc in next sc, work LDC, sc in next 2 sts, work LDC, sc in next LDC, work LDC, sc in next 2 sts, work LDC, ★ sc in next 13 sc, work LDC, sc in next 2 sts, work LDC, sc in next LDC, work LDC, sc in next 2 sts, work LDC; repeat from ★ across to last 2 sc, sc in last 2 sc; finish off: 44 LDC and 189 sc.

Row 9: Join next color with sc in first sc; work LDC, sc in next 2 sts, work LDC, sc in next 3 sts, work LDC, sc in next 2 sts, work LDC, ★ sc in next 11 sc, work LDC, sc in next 2 sts, work LDC, sc in next 3 sts, work LDC, sc in next 2 sts, work LDC; repeat from ★ across to last sc, sc in last sc; finish off.

Row 10: Join next color with sc in first sc; sc in next LDC, work Split LDC, sc in next 2 sts, work Split LDC, sc in next sc, work Split LDC, sc in next 2 sts, work Split LDC, ★ sc in next 13 sts, work Split LDC, sc in next 2 sts, work Split LDC, sc in next sc, work Split LDC, sc in next 2 sts, work Split LDC; repeat from ★ across to last 2 sts, sc in last 2 sts; finish off.

Row 11: Repeat Row 7.
Row 12: Repeat Row 6.
Row 13: Repeat Row 5.
Row 14: Repeat Row 4.
Row 15: Join next color with sc in first sc; sc in each st across; finish off: 233 sc.

Continued on page 110.

FOREST DREAM Continued from page 108.

Row 16: Join next color with sc in first sc; sc in next 16 sts, work LDC, ★ sc in next 21 sts, work LDC; repeat from ★ across to last 17 sts, sc in last 17 sts; finish off: 10 LDC and 223 sc.

Row 17: Join next color with sc in first sc; sc in next 15 sts, work LDC, sc in next st, work LDC, ★ sc in next 19 sts, work LDC, sc in next st, work LDC; repeat from ★ across to last 16 sts, sc in last 16 sts; finish off: 20 LDC and 213 sc.

Row 18: Join next color with sc in first sc; sc in next 14 sts, work LDC, sc in next 3 sts, work LDC, ★ sc in next 17 sts, work LDC, sc in next 3 sts, work LDC; repeat from ★ across to last 15 sts, sc in last 15 sts; finish off.

Row 19: Join next color with sc in first sc; sc in next 13 sts, work LDC, (sc in next 2 sts, work LDC) twice, ★ sc in next 15 sts, work LDC, (sc in next 2 sts, work LDC) twice; repeat from ★ across to last 14 sts, sc in last 14 sts; finish off: 30 LDC and 203 sc.

Row 20: Join next color with sc in first sc; sc in next 12 sc, ★ work LDC, sc in next 2 sts, work LDC, sc in next LDC, work LDC, sc in next 2 sts, work LDC, sc in next 13 sc; repeat from ★ across; finish off: 40 LDC and 193 sc.

Row 21: Join next color with sc in first sc; ★ sc in next 11 sc, work LDC, sc in next 2 sts, work LDC, sc in next 3 sts, work LDC, sc in next 2 sts, work LDC; repeat from ★ across to last 12 sc, sc in last 12 sc; finish off.

Row 22: Join next color with sc in first sc; sc in next 12 sts, ★ work Split LDC, sc in next 2 sts, work Split LDC, sc in next sc, work Split LDC, sc in next 2 sts, work Split LDC, sc in next 13 sts; repeat from ★ across; finish off.

Row 23: Repeat Row 19.
Row 24: Repeat Row 18.
Row 25: Repeat Row 17.
Row 26: Repeat Row 16.
Row 27: Join next color with sc in first sc; sc in each st across; finish off: 233 sc.
Rows 28-183: Repeat Rows 4-27, 6 times; then repeat Rows 4-15 once **more**.

Using corresponding color, add one strand of fringe to each row across short edges of Afghan *(Figs. 36b & d, page 142)*.

RADIANT MUMS Continued from page 102.

Rnd 6: Ch 3, dc in next dc, (2 dc, ch 2, 2 dc) in next ch-2 sp, ★ dc in each dc across to next ch-2 sp, (2 dc, ch 2, 2 dc) in ch-2 sp; repeat from ★ 2 times **more**, dc in each dc across; join with slip st to first dc, finish off: 104 dc.

ASSEMBLY
Using Off-White and working through inside loops only, whipstitch Squares together *(Fig. 35a, page 141)*, forming 6 vertical strips of 9 Squares each, beginning in second ch of first corner ch-2 and ending in first ch of next corner ch-2; whipstitch strips together in same manner.

EDGING
Rnd 1: With **right** side facing, join Off-White with slip st in any dc; ch 1, sc evenly around working 3 sc in each corner ch-2 sp; join with slip st to first sc.
Rnd 2: Ch 1, sc in same st and in each sc around working 3 sc in center sc of each corner; join with slip st to first sc, finish off.

BLUE RIBBON WINNER Continued from page 104.

Rnd 2: With **right** side facing, join Lt Blue with slip st in any corner ch-2 sp; work (beginning Popcorn, ch 4, Popcorn) in same sp, ch 3, (skip next 2 sc, work Popcorn in next sc, ch 3) 6 times, skip next 2 sc, ★ work (Popcorn, ch 4, Popcorn) in next corner ch-2 sp, ch 3, (skip next 2 sc, work Popcorn in next sc, ch 3) 6 times, skip next 2 sc; repeat from ★ around; join with slip st to top of beginning Popcorn, finish off: 32 sps.

Rnd 3: With **right** side facing, join Blue with slip st in any corner ch-4 sp; ch 3, (2 dc, ch 3, 3 dc) in same sp, ch 1, (3 dc in next ch-3 sp, ch 1) 7 times, ★ (3 dc, ch 3, 3 dc) in next corner ch-4 sp, ch 1, (3 dc in next ch-3 sp, ch 1) 7 times; repeat from ★ around; join with slip st to first dc, finish off: 36 sps.

Rnd 4: With **right** side facing, join Dk Blue with slip st in any corner ch-3 sp; ch 3, (2 dc, ch 3, 3 dc) in same sp, ch 1, (3 dc in next ch-1 sp, ch 1) 8 times, ★ (3 dc, ch 3, 3 dc) in next corner ch-3 sp, ch 1, (3 dc in next ch-1 sp, ch 1) 8 times; repeat from ★ around; join with slip st to first dc, finish off: 120 dc and 40 sps.

ASSEMBLY

Using Dk Blue, and working through both loops, whipstitch Squares together, *(Fig. 35b, page 141)*, forming 5 vertical strips of 7 Squares each, beginning in center ch of first corner and ending in center ch of next corner; whipstitch strips together in same manner.

EDGING

With **right** side facing, join Dk Blue with slip st in any corner ch-3 sp; ch 3, (2 dc, ch 3, 3 dc) in same sp, ★ † ch 1, (3 dc in next ch-1 sp, ch 1) 9 times, [2 dc in next sp, dc in next joining, 2 dc in next sp, ch 1, (3 dc in next ch-1 sp, ch 1) 9 times] across to next corner ch-3 sp †, (3 dc, ch 3, 3 dc) in ch-3 sp; repeat from ★ 2 times **more**, then repeat from † to † once; join with slip st to first dc, finish off.

Holding six strands of Dk Blue together, add fringe evenly across short edges of Afghan *(Figs. 36a & c, page 142)*.

BOW TIES Continued from page 106.

Rnd 3: Slip st in next sc, 3 hdc in next sc, (skip next sc, slip st in next sc, 3 hdc in next sc) 4 times, (slip st in next sc, skip next LDC, 3 hdc in sp **before** next LDC) 52 times, (skip next sc, slip st in next sc, 3 hdc in next sc) 5 times, (slip st in next sc, skip next LDC, 3 hdc in sp **before** next LDC) across; join with slip st to first slip st, finish off: 114 3-hdc groups.

Rnd 4: With **right** side facing, join Green with slip st in second hdc to **right** of joining; ch 3, skip next 3 sts, slip st in next hdc, (ch 4, skip next 3 sts, slip st in next hdc) 4 times, (ch 3, skip next 3 sts, slip st in next hdc) 53 times, (ch 4, skip next 3 sts, slip st in next hdc) 4 times, ch 3, (skip next 3 sts, slip st in next hdc, ch 3) across; join with slip st to first slip st: 114 sps.

Rnd 5: Slip st in first ch-3 sp, ch 3 (**counts as first dc**), 2 dc in same sp, † 3 dc in next ch-4 sp, place marker around last dc made for joining placement, 4 dc in same sp, 7 dc in each of next 2 ch-4 sps, 5 dc in next ch-4 sp, place marker around last dc made for joining placement, 2 dc in same sp †, 3 dc in each of next 5 ch-3 sps, (4 dc in next ch-3 sp, 3 dc in each of next 5 ch-3 sps) 8 times, repeat from † to † once, (3 dc in each of next 5 ch-3 sps, 4 dc in next ch-3 sp) across to last 4 ch-3 sps, 3 dc in each of last 4 ch-3 sps; join with slip st to first dc, finish off.

ASSEMBLY

Place two Strips with **wrong** sides together and bottom edges at the same end. Using Green and working through inside loops only, whipstitch Strips together *(Fig. 35a, page 141)*, beginning in first marked dc and ending in last marked dc, do **not** remove markers on first and last Strip.

Join remaining Strips in same manner, always working in same direction.

EDGING

Rnd 1: With **right** side facing, join Ecru with sc in marked dc at top right edge, remove marker; sc in next 4 dc, † 2 sc in next dc, (sc in next 5 dc, 2 sc in next dc) twice, ★ sc in next 4 dc, decrease, sc in next 3 dc, 2 sc in next dc, (sc in next 5 dc, 2 sc in next dc) twice; repeat from ★ 7 times **more** †, sc in each dc across to second marked dc, sc in marked dc and in next 4 dc, remove all markers, repeat from † to † once, sc in each dc across; join with slip st to first dc.

Rnd 2: Ch 1, working from **left** to **right**, ★ work reverse sc in each sc across to within one sc of next decrease, skip next sc, work reverse sc in decrease, skip next sc; repeat from ★ 15 times **more**, work reverse sc in each sc around; join with slip st to first st, finish off.

HANDSOME RIPPLE

Fashioned in the earthy tones that gentlemen prefer, this handsome afghan is especially well suited for a den or office. The timeless ripple, worked using clusters and V-stitches, is steeped with tradition.

Finished Size: 48" x 64"

MATERIALS

Worsted Weight Yarn:
Brown - 19 ounces,
   (540 grams, 1,250 yards)
Gold - 4 ounces,
   (110 grams, 265 yards)
Lt Gold - 8 ounces,
   (230 grams, 525 yards)
Ecru - 6 ounces,
   (170 grams, 395 yards)
Crochet hook, size H (5.00 mm) **or** size
   needed for gauge

GAUGE: One repeat from point to point
   and 8 rows = 4"

Gauge Swatch: 8¹/₂"w x 4"h
Ch 41 **loosely**.
Work same as Afghan for 8 rows.
Finish off.

STITCH GUIDE

> **V-ST**
> (Dc, ch 1, dc) in st indicated.
> **CLUSTER** (uses next 5 sts)
> YO, insert hook in **next** st, YO and pull up a loop, YO and
> draw through 2 loops on hook, ★ YO, skip **next** st, insert
> hook in **next** st, YO and pull up a loop, YO and draw through
> 2 loops on hook; repeat from ★ once **more**, YO and draw
> through all 4 loops on hook *(Figs. 17c & d, page 136)*.

COLOR SEQUENCE

8 Rows Brown *(Fig. 31a, page 139)*, ★ 3 rows Gold, one row
Brown, 3 rows Lt Gold, one row Gold, 3 rows Ecru,
one row Lt Gold, 8 rows Brown; repeat from ★ throughout.

With Brown, ch 221 **loosely**.

Row 1 (Right side)**:** Dc in fifth ch from hook **(4 skipped chs
count as first dc plus ch 1)**, (skip next ch, work V-St in next
ch) twice, skip next 2 chs, work Cluster, ★ skip next 2 chs,
(work V-St in next ch, skip next ch) twice, dc in next ch, (ch 1,
dc in same st) twice, (skip next ch, work V-St in next ch) twice,
skip next 2 chs, work Cluster; repeat from ★ 10 times **more**,
skip next 2 chs, work V-St in next ch, (skip next ch, work V-St in
next ch) twice: 145 sts and 72 ch-1 sps.
Note: Loop a short piece of yarn around any stitch to mark
Row 1 as **right** side.
Row 2: Ch 1, turn; sc in each st and in each ch-1 sp across:
217 sc.
Row 3: Ch 4 **(counts as first dc plus ch 1)**, turn; dc in same
st, (skip next sc, work V-St in next sc) twice, skip next 2 sc,
work Cluster, ★ skip next 2 sc, (work V-St in next sc, skip next
sc) twice, dc in next sc, (ch 1, dc in same st) twice, (skip next
sc, work V-St in next sc) twice, skip next 2 sc, work Cluster;
repeat from ★ 10 times **more**, skip next 2 sc, work V-St in next
sc, (skip next sc, work V-St in next sc) twice.
Row 4: Ch 1, turn; sc in each st and in each ch-1 sp across.
Repeat Rows 3 and 4 until Afghan measures 64" from beginning
ch, ending by working 8 rows Brown.
Finish off.

Holding 12 strands of Brown together, add fringe at each point
across short edges of Afghan *(Figs. 36a & c, page 142)*.

FALLING LEAVES

The motifs on this resplendent wrap remind us of the spectacular golden hues of falling leaves. The rich-toned throw, worked in squares of worsted weight yarn, will add a warm glow to your home.

Finished Size: 46" x 64"

MATERIALS
Worsted Weight Yarn:
  Tan - 5½ ounces, (160 grams, 360 yards)
  Lt Brown - 10½ ounces, (300 grams, 690 yards)
  Brown - 10 ounces, (280 grams, 655 yards)
  Dk Brown - 20 ounces, (570 grams, 1,315 yards)
Crochet hook, size H (5.00 mm) **or** size needed
  for gauge
Yarn needle

GAUGE: Each Square = 9"

Gauge Swatch: 4"
Work same as Square through Rnd 3.

STITCH GUIDE

> **LONG TREBLE CROCHET (abbreviated LTR)**
> YO twice, working around ch-1 sp on Rnd 4 **and** dc on Rnd 3, insert hook in sp indicated on Rnd 2, YO and pull up a loop, (YO and draw through 2 loops on hook) 3 times *(Fig. 20, page 137)*.

SQUARE (Make 35)

With Tan, ch 6; join with slip st to form a ring.

Rnd 1 (Right side): Ch 3 **(counts as first dc, now and throughout)**, 2 dc in ring, ch 3, (3 dc in ring, ch 3) 3 times; join with slip st to first dc, finish off: 4 ch-3 sps.

Note: Loop a short piece of yarn around any stitch to mark Rnd 1 as **right** side.

Rnd 2: With **wrong** side facing, join Lt Brown with slip st in any ch-3 sp; ch 3, 8 dc in same sp, ch 1, (9 dc in next ch-3 sp, ch 1) around; join with slip st to first dc: 36 dc and 4 ch-1 sps.

Rnd 3: Turn; slip st in first ch-1 sp, ch 3, 2 dc in same sp, ch 1, skip next 4 dc, 9 dc in next dc, ch 1, ★ 3 dc in next ch-1 sp, ch 1, skip next 4 dc, 9 dc in next dc, ch 1; repeat from ★ around; join with slip st to first dc, finish off: 48 dc and 8 ch-1 sps.

Rnd 4: With **wrong** side facing, join Brown with slip st in center dc of any 9-dc group; ch 3, 8 dc in same st, ch 1, (3 dc in next ch-1 sp, ch 1) twice, skip next 4 dc, ★ 9 dc in next dc, ch 1, (3 dc in next ch-1 sp, ch 1) twice, skip next 4 dc; repeat from ★ around; join with slip st to first dc, finish off: 60 dc and 12 ch-1 sps.

Rnd 5: With **wrong** side facing, join Dk Brown with slip st in center dc of any 9-dc group; ch 4 **(counts as first dc plus ch 1)**, (dc in same st, ch 1) 4 times, 3 tr in next ch-1 sp, ch 1, work 3 LTR in next ch-1 sp on Rnd 2, ch 1, 3 tr in next ch-1 sp on Rnd 4, ch 1, skip next 4 dc, ★ (dc, ch 1) 5 times in next dc, 3 tr in next ch-1 sp, ch 1, work 3 LTR in next ch-1 sp on Rnd 2, ch 1, 3 tr in next ch-1 sp on Rnd 4, ch 1, skip next 4 dc; repeat from ★ around; join with slip st to first dc, finish off: 56 sts and 32 ch-1 sps.

Continued on page 121.

INDIAN SUMMER

The beautiful days of Indian summer inspired this dramatic wrap, which is crocheted in colors reflecting the crisp blue skies and burnt-orange leaves of autumn. The rippled throw is worked using single crochets.

Finished Size: 49" x 62"

MATERIALS

Worsted Weight Yarn:
- Black - 14 ounces, (400 grams, 880 yards)
- Rust - 10 ounces, (280 grams, 630 yards)
- Ecru - 18 ounces, (510 grams, 1,130 yards)
- Teal - 9 ounces, (260 grams, 565 yards)

Crochet hook, size H (5.00 mm) **or** size needed for gauge

GAUGE: In pattern 3 repeats (point to point) = 5¼" and 8 rows = 3"

Gauge Swatch: 7"w x 3"h
Ch 39 **loosely**.
Work same as Afghan for 8 rows.
Finish off.

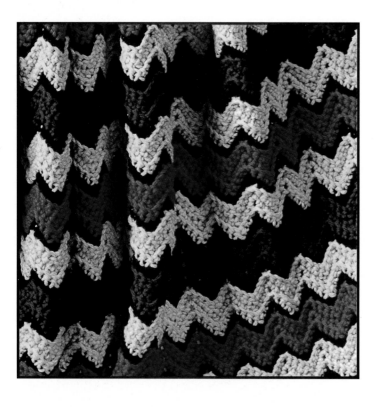

STITCH GUIDE

DECREASE
Pull up a loop in next 2 sc, YO and draw through all 3 loops on hook **(counts as one sc)**.

COLOR SEQUENCE

One row Black *(Fig. 31a, page 139)*, 3 rows Rust, one row Black, ★ 3 rows Ecru, one row Black, 3 rows Teal, one row Black, 3 rows Ecru, one row Black, 3 rows Rust, one row Black; repeat from ★ throughout.

With Black, ch 255 **loosely**.

Row 1 (Right side)**:** Sc in second ch from hook and in next 4 chs, 3 sc in next ch, ★ sc in next 3 chs, skip next 2 chs, sc in next 3 chs, 3 sc in next ch; repeat from ★ across to last 5 chs, sc in last 5 chs: 256 sc.

Row 2: Ch 1, turn; working in Back Loops Only *(Fig. 28, page 139)*, decrease, sc in next 4 sc, 3 sc in next sc, ★ sc in next 3 sc, skip next 2 sc, sc in next 3 sc, 3 sc in next sc; repeat from ★ across to last 6 sc, sc in next 4 sc, decrease: 256 sc.
Repeat Row 2 until Afghan measures 62" from beginning ch, ending by working one row Black.
Finish off.

APPEALING PINEAPPLES

There's nothing more inviting than a comfortable chair draped with a cozy afghan. This mile-a-minute throw is especially welcoming because it features pineapple motifs — traditional symbols of hospitality.

Finished Size: 57" x 71"

MATERIALS

Worsted Weight Yarn:
   52 ounces, (1,480 grams, 3,415 yards)
Crochet hook, size I (5.50 mm) **or** size needed
   for gauge
Yarn needle

GAUGE: Each Strip = 7" wide

Gauge Swatch: 4¼"w x 4½"h
Work same as Center for 8 rows.

STITCH GUIDE

DOUBLE TREBLE CLUSTER
(abbreviated dtr Cluster)
★ YO 3 times, insert hook in st indicated, YO and pull up a loop, (YO and draw through 2 loops on hook) 3 times; repeat from ★ 2 times **more**, YO and draw through all 4 loops on hook *(Figs. 17a & b, page 136)*.

TREBLE CROCHET CLUSTER
(abbreviated tr Cluster)
★ YO twice, insert hook in st indicated, YO and pull up a loop, (YO and draw through 2 loops on hook) twice; repeat from ★ 2 times **more**, YO and draw through all 4 loops on hook.

DOUBLE CROCHET CLUSTER
(abbreviated dc Cluster)
★ YO, insert hook in st indicated, YO and pull up a loop, YO and draw through 2 loops on hook; repeat from ★ 2 times **more**, YO and draw through all 4 loops on hook.

DECREASE
Insert hook in same st as joining on **same** Strip and pull up a loop, insert hook in same st as joining on **next** Strip and pull up a loop, YO and draw through all 3 loops on hook.

STRIP (Make 8)
CENTER
Ch 6; join with slip st to form a ring.

Row 1 (Right side): Ch 4 **(counts as first tr, now and throughout)**, 9 tr in ring: 10 tr.

Note: Loop a short piece of yarn around any stitch to mark Row 1 as **right** side and bottom edge.

Row 2: Ch 1, turn; skip first tr, sc in sp **before** next tr **(Fig. 33, page 140)**, ★ ch 3, skip next tr, sc in sp **before** next tr; repeat from ★ across: 8 ch-3 sps.

Rows 3-8: Turn; slip st in first ch-3 sp, ch 1, sc in same sp, (ch 3, sc in next ch-3 sp) across: 2 ch-3 sps.

Row 9: Turn; slip st in first ch-3 sp, ch 1, sc in same sp, ch 3, sc in last ch-3 sp: one ch-3 sp.

Row 10: Turn; slip st in first ch-3 sp, ch 4, 9 tr in same sp: 10 tr.

Rows 11-126: Repeat Rows 2-10, 12 times; then repeat Rows 2-9 once **more**; do **not** finish off: one ch-3 sp.

BORDER
Rnd 1: Turn; slip st in first ch-3 sp, ch 1, 7 sc in same sp; working in end of rows, 2 sc in each of next 7 rows, 4 sc in next row, ★ sc in next row, 2 sc in each of next 7 rows, 4 sc in next row; repeat from ★ 12 times **more**, 3 sc in beginning ch-6 ring; working in end of rows, 4 sc in next row, 2 sc in each of next 7 rows, † sc in next row, 4 sc in next row, 2 sc in each of next 7 rows †, repeat from † to † across; join with slip st to first sc: 540 sc.

Rnd 2: Ch 1, do **not** turn; sc in same st, ch 3, (skip next sc, sc in next sc, ch 3) 8 times, skip next 2 sc, sc in next sc, ch 3, skip next sc, sc in next sc, † ch 3, skip next 6 sc, sc in next sc, ★ ch 3, (skip next sc, sc in next sc, ch 3) 6 times, skip next 6 sc, sc in next sc; repeat from ★ 11 times **more** †, (ch 3, skip next sc, sc in next sc) 17 times, repeat from † to † once, ch 3, skip next sc, sc in next sc, ch 3, skip next 2 sc, (sc in next sc, ch 3, skip next sc) 5 times; join with slip st to first sc: 204 ch-3 sps.

Continued on page 120.

APPEALING PINEAPPLES Continued from page 118.

Rnd 3: Slip st in first ch-3 sp, ch 1, 2 sc in same sp, 3 sc in next ch-3 sp, † 2 sc in each of next 6 ch-3 sps, 3 sc in next ch-3 sp †, 2 sc in next ch-3 sp, 3 sc in next ch-3 sp, repeat from † to † 12 times, 2 sc in each of next 4 ch-3 sps, 3 sc in next ch-3 sp, (2 sc in next ch-3 sp, 3 sc in next ch-3 sp) 4 times, 2 sc in each of next 4 ch-3 sps, 3 sc in next ch 3 sp, repeat from † to † 12 times, 2 sc in next ch-3 sp, 3 sc in next ch-3 sp, 2 sc in each of last 5 ch-3 sps; join with slip st to first sc: 442 sc.

Rnd 4: Slip st in next sc, ch 1, sc in same st and in next 4 sc, ch 4, skip next 4 sc, work (dtr Cluster, ch 5, tr Cluster) in next sc, ch 4, skip next 4 sc, sc in next 5 sc, ch 4, skip next 4 sc, work (dc Cluster, ch 2, dc Cluster) in next sc, ch 4, ★ skip next 4 sc, sc in next 5 sc, ch 4, skip next 5 sc, work (dc Cluster, ch 2, dc Cluster) in next sc, ch 4; repeat from ★ 11 times **more**, skip next 4 sc, sc in next 6 sc, ch 3, skip next 3 sc, work (dc Cluster, ch 5, dc Cluster) in next sc, ch 3, skip next 2 sc, sc in next 7 sc, ch 3, skip next 2 sc, work (dc Cluster, ch 5, dc Cluster) in next sc, ch 3, skip next 3 sc, sc in next 6 sc, † ch 4, skip next 4 sc, work (dc Cluster, ch 2, dc Cluster) in next sc, ch 4, skip next 5 sc, sc in next 5 sc †, repeat from † to † 12 times **more**, ch 4, skip next 3 sc, work (tr Cluster, ch 5, dtr Cluster) in next sc, ch 4, skip last 4 sc; join with slip st to first sc: 154 sc and 90 sps.

Rnd 5: Ch 3 **(counts as first dc)**, dc in next 4 sc, 5 dc in next ch-4 sp, (dc in next st, 5 dc in next sp) twice, † dc in next 5 sc, 4 dc in next ch-4 sp, dc in next st, 2 dc in next ch-2 sp, dc in next st, 4 dc in next ch-4 sp †, repeat from † to † 12 times **more**, dc in next 6 sc, 3 dc in next ch-3 sp, dc in next st, 5 dc in next sp, dc in next st, 3 dc in next ch-3 sp, dc in next 7 sc, 3 dc in next ch-3 sp, dc in next st, 5 dc in next sp, dc in next st, 3 dc in next ch-3 sp, dc in next 6 sc, ★ 4 dc in next ch-4 sp, dc in next st, 2 dc in next ch-2 sp, dc in next st, 4 dc in next ch-4 sp, dc in next 5 sc; repeat from ★ 12 times **more**, 5 dc in next ch-4 sp, (dc in next st, 5 dc in next sp) twice; join with slip st to first dc, finish off: 526 dc.

ASSEMBLY

Place two Strips with **wrong** sides together and bottom edges at same end. Working through inside loops only, whipstitch Strips together **(Fig. 35a, page 141)**, beginning in center dc of first corner 5-dc group and ending in center dc of next corner 5-dc group.

Join remaining Strips in same manner, always working in same direction.

EDGING

With **right** side facing and working in Back Loops Only **(Fig. 28, page 139)**, join yarn with slip st in any dc; ch 1, sc in same st and in each dc around, decreasing at each joining; join with slip st to first sc, finish off.

Rnd 6: With **right** side facing, join Tan with slip st in center dc of any corner; ch 6 **(counts as first dc plus ch 3, now and throughout)**, dc in same st, ch 1, (dc in next ch-1 sp, ch 1) 3 times, skip next tr, dc in next tr, ch 1, (dc in next ch-1 sp, ch 1, skip next st, dc in next st, ch 1) twice, (dc in next ch-1 sp, ch 1) 3 times, ★ (dc, ch 3, dc) in next dc, ch 1, (dc in next ch-1 sp, ch 1) 3 times, skip next tr, dc in next tr, ch 1, (dc in next ch-1 sp, ch 1, skip next st, dc in next st, ch 1) twice, (dc in next ch-1 sp, ch 1) 3 times; repeat from ★ around; join with slip st to first dc, finish off: 52 dc and 4 ch-3 sps.

Rnd 7: With **wrong** side facing, join Lt Brown with slip st in any ch-3 sp; ch 6, dc in same sp, ch 1, (dc in next dc, ch 1) across to next ch-3 sp, ★ (dc, ch 3, dc) in ch-3 sp, ch 1, (dc in next dc, ch 1) across to next ch-3 sp; repeat from ★ around; join with slip st to first dc, finish off: 60 dc.

Rnd 8: With **right** side facing, join Brown with slip st in any ch-3 sp; ch 6, dc in same sp, ch 1, (dc in next dc, ch 1) across to next ch-3 sp, ★ (dc, ch 3, dc) in ch-3 sp, ch 1, (dc in next dc, ch 1) across to next ch-3 sp; repeat from ★ around; join with slip st to first dc, finish off: 68 dc.

Rnd 9: With **right** side facing, join Dk Brown with slip st in any ch-3 sp; ch 1, (sc, ch 3, sc) in same sp, ch 1, (sc in next dc, ch 1) across to next ch-3 sp, ★ (sc, ch 3, sc) in ch-3 sp, ch 1, (sc in next dc, ch 1) across to next ch-3 sp; repeat from ★ around; join with slip st to first sc, finish off: 76 sc.

ASSEMBLY

Using Dk Brown, and working through both loops, whipstitch Squares together *(Fig. 35b, page 141)*, forming 5 vertical strips of 7 Squares each, beginning in center ch of first corner and ending in center ch of next corner; whipstitch strips together in same manner.

EDGING

With **right** side facing, join Dk Brown with slip st in any sc; ch 1, sc evenly around working (sc, ch 3, sc) in each corner ch-3 sp; join with slip st to first sc, finish off.

Holding 4 strands of Dk Brown together, add fringe evenly across short edges of Afghan *(Figs. 36a & c, page 142)*.

BUFFALO PLAID

Squares of red, black, and a combination of the two give this dramatic wrap rich color and texture. The buffalo plaid throw works up quickly using a large hook and holding two strands of yarn together.

STITCH GUIDE

DECREASE (uses next 2 sps)
Pull up a loop in next 2 sps, YO and draw through all 3 loops on hook **(counts as one sc)**.
REVERSE SINGLE CROCHET
Working from **left** to **right**, ★ insert hook in st to right of hook, YO and draw through, under, and to left of loop on hook (2 loops on hook), YO and draw through both loops on hook **(reverse sc made)**; repeat from ★ around **(Figs. 27a-d, page 138)**.

SQUARE A (Make 10)

With one strand of Black and one strand of Red held together, ch 5; join with slip st to form a ring.

Rnd 1 (Right side): Ch 6 **(counts as first dc plus ch 3, now and throughout)**, (3 dc in ring, ch 3) 3 times, 2 dc in ring; join with slip st to first dc: 12 dc and 4 ch-3 sps.

Note: Loop a short piece of yarn around any stitch to mark Rnd 1 as **right** side.

Rnds 2-5: Slip st in first corner ch-3 sp, ch 6, 2 dc in same sp, dc in each dc across to next corner ch-3 sp, ★ (2 dc, ch 3, 2 dc) in corner ch-3 sp, dc in each dc across to next corner ch-3 sp; repeat from ★ 2 times **more**, dc in same sp as first dc; join with slip st to first dc: 76 dc.
Finish off.

SQUARE B (Make 6)

With 2 strands of Black held together, ch 5; join with slip st to form a ring.
Complete same as Square A.

SQUARE C (Make 4)

With 2 strands of Red held together, ch 5; join with slip st to form a ring.
Complete same as Square A.

Continued on page 131.

Finished Size: 49" x 61"

MATERIALS
   Worsted Weight Yarn:
      Black - 28 ounces,
         (800 grams, 1,585 yards)
      Red - 22½ ounces,
         (640 grams, 1,265 yards)
   Crochet hook, size Q (15.00 mm)
   Yarn needle

GAUGE: Rnds 1 and 2 = 4¾"
      Each Square = 12"

CHRISTMAS EVE

*This festive throw has all the charm of a gaily wrapped package!
The Christmasy afghan is a thoughtful keepsake gift, or make
it for yourself to enhance your own holiday celebrations.*

Finished Size: 54" x 69"

MATERIALS

Worsted Weight Yarn:

Red - 18½ ounces, (530 grams, 1,165 yards)

White - 11½ ounces, (330 grams, 725 yards)

Green - 23 ounces, (650 grams, 1,445 yards)

Crochet hook, size I (5.50 mm) **or** size needed
for gauge

Yarn needle

GAUGE: Each Square = 7½"

Gauge Swatch: 3½" in diameter.
Work same as Square through Rnd 2.

STITCH GUIDE

BEGINNING CLUSTER

Ch 2, ★ YO, insert hook in **same** sp, YO and pull up a loop,
YO and draw through 2 loops on hook; repeat from ★ once
more, YO and draw through all 3 loops on hook
(Figs. 17a & b, page 136).

CLUSTER

★ YO, insert hook in sp or st indicated, YO and pull up a
loop, YO and draw through 2 loops on hook; repeat from ★
2 times **more**, YO and draw through all 4 loops on hook.

3-DC CLUSTER (uses next 3 dc)

★ YO, insert hook in **next** dc, YO and pull up a loop, YO and
draw through 2 loops on hook; repeat from ★ 2 times **more**,
YO and draw through all 4 loops on hook **(Figs. 17c & d,
page 136)**.

SQUARE (Make 63)

With Red, ch 5; join with slip st to form a ring.

Rnd 1 (Right side)**:** Ch 4, (dc in ring, ch 1) 11 times; join with
slip st to third ch of beginning ch-4: 12 ch-1 sps.

Note: Loop a short piece of yarn around any stitch to mark
Rnd 1 as **right** side.

Rnd 2: Slip st in first ch-1 sp, work beginning Cluster, ch 3,
(work Cluster in next ch-1 sp, ch 3) around; join with slip st to
top of beginning Cluster, finish off: 12 ch-3 sps.

Rnd 3: With **right** side facing, join White with slip st in any
ch-3 sp; ch 1, sc in same sp, ch 5, (sc in next ch-3 sp, ch 5)
around; join with slip st to first sc, finish off: 12 ch-5 sps.

Rnd 4: With **right** side facing, join Green with slip st in any
ch-5 sp; ch 4, (3 tr, ch 3, 4 tr) in same sp (corner made), sc in
next ch-5 sp, ch 5, sc in next ch-5 sp, ★ (4 tr, ch 3, 4 tr) in next
ch-5 sp (corner made), sc in next ch-5 sp, ch 5, sc in next
ch-5 sp; repeat from ★ around; join with slip st to top of
beginning ch, finish off: 4 ch-3 sps and 4 ch-5 sps.

Rnd 5: With **right** side facing, join White with slip st in any
corner ch-3 sp; ch 3 **(counts as first dc, now and
throughout)**, (2 dc, ch 3, 3 dc) in same sp, ch 2, skip next
2 tr, 3 dc in next tr, ch 2, 3 dc in next ch-5 sp, ch 2, skip next
2 sts, 3 dc in next tr, ch 2, ★ (3 dc, ch 3, 3 dc) in next corner
ch-3 sp, ch 2, skip next 2 tr, 3 dc in next tr, ch 2, 3 dc in next
ch-5 sp, ch 2, skip next 2 sts, 3 dc in next tr, ch 2; repeat from
★ around; join with slip st to first dc, finish off: 60 dc.

Rnd 6: With **right** side facing, join Red with slip st in any
corner ch-3 sp; ch 3, (2 dc, ch 3, 3 dc) in same sp, ch 1, (3 dc
in next ch-2 sp, ch 1) across to next corner ch-3 sp, ★ (3 dc,
ch 3, 3 dc) in ch-3 sp, ch 1, (3 dc in next ch-2 sp, ch 1) across
to next corner ch-3 sp; repeat from ★ around; join with slip st
to first dc, finish off: 72 dc.

Rnd 7: With **right** side facing, join Green with slip st in any
corner ch-3 sp; ch 3, (2 dc, ch 3, 3 dc) in same sp, ch 1, (3 dc
in next ch-1 sp, ch 1) across to next corner ch-3 sp, ★ (3 dc,
ch 3, 3 dc) in ch-3 sp, ch 1, (3 dc in next ch-1 sp, ch 1) across
to next corner ch-3 sp; repeat from ★ around; join with slip st
to first dc, finish off: 84 dc and 28 sps.

Continued on page 131.

SNOW CRYSTALS

The motifs on this wintry wrap capture the magnificent beauty of snow crystals. A flowing fringe adds appeal.

Finished Size: 48" x 64"

MATERIALS

Worsted Weight Yarn:
Blue - 26 ounces, (740 grams, 1,635 yards)
White - 27 ounces, (770 grams, 1,695 yards)
Crochet hook, size J (6.00 mm) **or** size needed for gauge
Yarn needle

GAUGE: Each Square = 5¼"

SQUARE (Make 108)

With White, ch 6; join with slip st to form a ring.

Rnd 1 (Right side): Ch 1, 16 sc in ring; join with slip st to first sc.

Note: Loop a short piece of yarn around any stitch to mark Rnd 1 as **right** side.

Rnd 2: Ch 5 **(counts as first dc plus ch 2)**, dc in same st, ch 1, skip next sc, ★ (dc, ch 2, dc) in next sc, ch 1, skip next sc; repeat from ★ around; join with slip st to first dc: 16 sps.

Rnd 3: Slip st in first ch-2 sp, ch 2 **(counts as first hdc)**, (hdc, ch 2, 2 hdc) in same sp, sc in next ch-1 sp, ★ (2 hdc, ch 2, 2 hdc) in next ch-2 sp, sc in next ch-1 sp; repeat from ★ around; join with slip st to first hdc: 8 ch-2 sps.

Rnd 4: Slip st in next hdc and in next ch-2 sp, ch 3 **(counts as first dc)**, (2 dc, ch 1, 3 dc) in same sp, (3 dc, ch 1, 3 dc) in each ch-2 sp around; join with slip st to first dc, finish off: 48 dc and 8 ch-1 sps.

Rnd 5: With **right** side facing, join Blue with slip st in any ch-1 sp; ch 7 **(counts as first tr plus ch 3)**, tr in same sp and in next 3 dc, dc in next dc, hdc in next dc, sc in next dc, sc in next ch-1 sp and in next dc, hdc in next dc, dc in next dc, tr in next 3 dc, ★ (tr, ch 3, tr) in next ch-1 sp, tr in next 3 dc, dc in next dc, hdc in next dc, sc in next dc, sc in next ch-1 sp and in next dc, hdc in next dc, dc in next dc, tr in next 3 dc; repeat from ★ around; join with slip st to first tr, finish off: 60 sts and 4 ch-3 sps.

ASSEMBLY

Using Blue and working through both loops, whipstitch Squares together *(Fig. 35b, page 141)*, forming 9 vertical strips of 12 Squares each, beginning in center ch of first corner and ending in center ch of next corner; whipstitch strips together in same manner.

EDGING

Rnd 1: With **right** side facing, join Blue with slip st in any st; ch 1, sc evenly around working 3 sc in each corner ch-3 sp; join with slip st to first sc.

Rnd 2: Ch 1, (slip st in next sc, ch 1) around; join with slip st to first slip st, finish off.

Holding 5 strands of Blue together, add fringe evenly across short edges of Afghan *(Figs. 36a & c, page 142)*.

DECKED WITH HOLLY

An heirloom in the making, this wrap is one that generations will enjoy using for many holidays to come. Trimmed with an elegant holly border, the afghan features a cozy allover pattern of puff stitches.

Finished Size: 54" x 72"

MATERIALS

Worsted Weight Yarn:
  Beige - 50 ounces, (1,420 grams, 3,145 yards)
  Green - 7 ounces, (200 grams, 440 yards)
  Red - 2 ounces, (60 grams, 125 yards)
Crochet hook, size H (5.00 mm) **or** size needed for gauge
Yarn needle

GAUGE: In pattern, 3 repeats = 4¼"
        and 10 rows = 4"

Gauge Swatch: 5¾"w x 4"h
Ch 26 **loosely**.
Work same as Center for 10 rows.
Finish off.

STITCH GUIDE

V-ST
(Dc, ch 2, dc) in st indicated.

PUFF ST
★ YO, insert hook in st indicated, YO and pull up a loop even with loop on hook; repeat from ★ 3 times **more**, YO and draw through all 9 loops on hook (*Fig. 19, page 137*).

DECREASE
Pull up a loop in next 2 sc, YO and draw through all 3 loops on hook (**counts as one sc**).

DOUBLE DECREASE
Pull up a loop in next 3 sc, YO and draw through all 4 loops on hook (**counts as one sc**).

CLUSTER (uses next 2 points)
YO twice, insert hook in **next** point, YO and pull up a loop, (YO and draw through 2 loops on hook) twice, YO twice, insert hook in first point on **next** Leaf, YO and pull up a loop, (YO and draw through 2 loops on hook) twice, YO and draw through all 3 loops on hook (*Figs. 17c & d, page 136*).

CENTER

With Beige, ch 200 **loosely**.

Row 1 (Right side)**:** Sc in second ch from hook, ★ ch 1, skip next 2 chs, work V-St in next ch, ch 1, skip next 2 chs, sc in next ch; repeat from ★ across: 33 V-Sts.

Note: Loop a short piece of yarn around any stitch to mark Row 1 as **right** side.

Row 2: Ch 5 (**counts as first dc plus ch 2**), turn; sc in next V-St (ch-2 sp), ch 2, ★ work Puff St in next sc, ch 3, sc in next V-St, ch 2; repeat from ★ across to last sc, dc in last sc: 32 Puff Sts and 66 sps.

Row 3: Ch 1, turn; sc in first dc, ch 1, work V-St in next sc, ch 1, ★ sc in next Puff St, ch 1, work V-St in next sc, ch 1; repeat from ★ across to last dc, sc in last dc.

Rows 4-164: Repeat Rows 2 and 3, 80 times; then repeat Row 2 once **more**; do **not** finish off.

EDGING

Ch 1, turn; (sc, ch 3) twice in first dc, skip next ch-2 sp, sc in next st, (ch 3, skip next sp, sc in next st) across to last ch-2 sp, place marker around last ch-3 made for joining placement, ch 3, skip last ch-2 sp, (sc, ch 3) twice in last dc; † working in end of rows, skip first row, (sc in next row, ch 3, skip next row) 10 times, (sc in next row, ch 3) twice, ★ skip next row, (sc in next row, ch 3, skip next row) 10 times, (sc in next row, ch 3) twice; repeat from ★ across to last 3 rows, skip next row, (sc in next row, ch 3) twice †; working in free loops of beginning ch (*Fig. 29b, page 139*), (sc, ch 3) twice in first ch, skip next 2 chs, (sc in next ch, ch 3, skip next 2 chs) across to ch at base of first sc, (sc, ch 3) twice in ch at base of first sc, repeat from † to † once; join with slip st to first sc, finish off: 310 ch-3 sps.

Continued on page 130.

HOLLY BORDER
LEAVES
GAUGE: Rows 1-12 (one leaf) = 2³/₄"

Row 1 (Right side): With Green, ch 2, 3 sc in second ch from hook.
Note: Mark Row 1 as **right** side.
Row 2: Ch 1, turn; sc in each sc across.
Row 3: Ch 1, turn; 2 sc in first sc, sc in next sc, 2 sc in last sc: 5 sc.
Row 4: Ch 1, turn; 3 sc in first sc, sc in next 3 sc, 3 sc in last sc: 9 sc.
Row 5: Turn; slip st in first 3 sc, ch 1, sc in same st and in next 4 sc, leave remaining 2 sc unworked: 5 sc.
Row 6: Ch 1, turn; 2 sc in first sc, sc in next 3 sc, 2 sc in last sc: 7 sc.
Row 7: Ch 1, turn; 3 sc in first sc, sc in next 5 sc, 3 sc in last sc: 11 sc.
Row 8: Turn; slip st in first 2 sc, ch 1, decrease, double decrease, decrease, leave remaining 2 sc unworked: 3 sc.
Row 9: Ch 1, turn; 2 sc in first sc, sc in next sc, 2 sc in last sc: 5 sc.
Row 10: Ch 1, turn; 3 sc in first sc, sc in next 3 sc, 3 sc in last sc: 9 sc.
Row 11: Turn; slip st in first 2 sc, ch 1, decrease, sc in next sc, decrease, leave remaining 2 sc unworked: 3 sc.
Row 12: Ch 1, turn; double decrease: 1 sc.
Row 13: Ch 1, turn; 3 sc in next sc.
Repeat Rows 2-13 until 92 Leaves are complete, ending by working Row 12; finish off leaving a long end for sewing.

TRIM
Rnd 1: With **right** side facing and working in end of rows at each point along one edge of Leaves, join Beige with slip st in second point (Row 7) on first Leaf; ch 6 **(counts as first dc plus ch 3)**, † work Cluster, ch 3, dc in next point, ch 3, [sc in next point, ch 3, working around Leaves, work (dc, ch 3) twice between Leaves, sc in next point, ch 3, dc in next point, ch 3, work Cluster, ch 3, dc in next point, ch 3] 9 times, sc in next point and in first point on next Leaf to form corner, ch 3, dc in next point, ch 3, work Cluster, ch 3, dc in next point, ch 3, [sc in next point, ch 3, working around Leaves, work (dc, ch 3) twice between Leaves, sc in next point, ch 3, dc in next point, ch 3, work Cluster, ch 3, dc in next point, ch 3] 12 times, sc in next point and in first point on next Leaf to form corner, ch 3 †, dc in next point, ch 3, repeat from † to † once; join with slip st to first dc: 310 ch-3 sps.
Rnd 2 (Joining rnd): Slip st in first ch-3 sp, ch 1, sc in same sp, ch 2, holding Center and Holly Border with **wrong** sides together, sc in marked ch-3 sp on Center Edging *(Fig. 32, page 140)*, ch 2, ★ sc in next ch-3 sp on Holly Border Trim, ch 2, sc in next ch-3 sp on Center Edging, ch 2; repeat from ★ around; join with slip st to first sc on Holly Border Trim, finish off.

BERRIES (Make 46)
With Red, ★ ch 4, 4 dc in fourth ch from hook, drop loop on hook, insert hook in top of beginning ch-4, hook dropped loop and draw through (Berry made); repeat from ★ 2 times **more**, ch 1; join with slip st to base of first Berry, finish off leaving a long end for sewing.
Beginning at corner intersection of Leaves, sew Berries to every other intersection of Leaves.

BUFFALO PLAID Continued from page 122.

ASSEMBLY

Using Placement Diagram as a guide, holding one strand of Black and one strand of Red together, and working through inside loops only, whipstitch Squares together *(Fig. 35a, page 141)*, beginning in center ch of first corner and ending in center ch of next corner, forming 4 vertical strips of 5 Squares each; whipstitch strips together in same manner.

EDGING

Rnd 1: With **right** side facing and using one strand of Black and one strand of Red held together, join yarn with sc in any corner ch-3 sp *(see Joining With Sc, page 139)*; 2 sc in same sp, sc in next 19 dc, (decrease, sc in next 19 dc) across to next corner ch-3 sp, ★ 3 sc in corner ch-3 sp, sc in next 19 dc, (decrease, sc in next 19 dc) across to next corner ch-3 sp; repeat from ★ 2 times **more**; join with slip st to first sc: 368 sc.

Rnd 2: Ch 1, working from **left** to **right**, work reverse sc in each sc around; join with slip st to first st, finish off.

PLACEMENT DIAGRAM

A	B	A	B
C	A	C	A
A	B	A	B
C	A	C	A
A	B	A	B

CHRISTMAS EVE Continued from page 124.

ASSEMBLY

Using Green and working through both loops, whipstitch Squares together, forming 7 vertical strips of 9 Squares each *(Fig. 35b, page 141)*, beginning in center ch of first corner and ending in center ch of next corner; whipstitch strips together in same manner.

EDGING

With **right** side facing, join Green with slip st in any corner ch-3 sp; ch 10, dc in same sp, ch 5, (work 3-dc Cluster, ch 5) 7 times, † work Cluster in next joining, ch 5, (work 3-dc Cluster, ch 5) 7 times †, repeat from † to † across to next corner ch-3 sp, ★ (dc, ch 7, dc) in ch-3 sp, ch 5, (work 3-dc Cluster, ch 5) 7 times, repeat from † to † across to next corner ch-3 sp; repeat from ★ around; join with slip st to third ch of beginning ch-10, finish off.

general instructions

BASIC INFORMATION

ABBREVIATIONS

BPdc	Back Post double crochet(s)
BPsc	Back Post single crochet(s)
BPtr	Back Post treble crochet(s)
ch(s)	chain(s)
dc	double crochet(s)
Dk	Dark
dtr	double treble crochet(s)
FPdc	Front Post double crochet(s)
FPdtr	Front Post double treble crochet(s)
FPhdc	Front Post half double crochet(s)
FPtr	Front Post treble crochet(s)
hdc	half double crochet(s)
LDC	Long double crochet(s)
LSC	Long single crochet(s)
Lt	Light
LTR	Long treble crochet(s)
Med	Medium
mm	millimeters
Rnd(s)	Round(s)
sc	single crochet(s)
sp(s)	space(s)
st(s)	stitch(es)
tr	treble crochet(s)
tr tr	triple treble crochet(s)
YO	yarn over

SYMBOLS

★ — work instructions following ★ as many **more** times as indicated in addition to the first time.

† to † — work all instructions from first † to second † **as many** times as specified.

( ) or [ ] — work enclosed instructions **as many** times as specified by the number immediately following **or** work all enclosed instructions in the stitch or space indicated **or** contains explanatory remarks.

TERMS

chain loosely — work the chain **only** loose enough for the hook to pass through the chain easily when working the next row or round into the chain.

multiple — the number of stitches required to complete one repeat of a pattern.

post — the vertical shaft of a stitch.

right side vs. wrong side — the right side of your work is the side that will show when the piece is finished.

work across or around — continue working in the established pattern.

GAUGE

Gauge is the number of stitches and rows or rounds per inch and is used to determine the finished size of a project. All crochet patterns specify the gauge that you must match to ensure proper size and to ensure that you will have enough yarn to complete the project.

Hook size given in instructions is merely a guide. Because everyone crochets differently — loosely, tightly, or somewhere in between — the finished size can vary, even when crocheters use the very same pattern, yarn, and hook.

Before beginning any crocheted item, it is absolutely necessary for you to crochet a gauge swatch in the pattern stitch indicated and with the weight of yarn and hook size suggested. Your swatch must be large enough to measure your gauge. Lay your swatch on a hard, smooth, flat surface. Then measure it, counting your stitches and rows or rounds carefully. If your swatch is smaller than specified or you have too many stitches per inch, try again with a larger size hook; if your swatch is larger than specified or you don't have enough stitches per inch, try again with a smaller size hook. Keep trying until you find the size that will give you the specified gauge. DO NOT HESITATE TO CHANGE HOOK SIZE TO OBTAIN CORRECT GAUGE. Once proper gauge is obtained, measure width of piece approximately every 3" to be sure gauge remains consistent.

BASIC STITCH GUIDE

CHAIN *(abbreviated ch)*

To work a chain stitch, begin with a slip knot on the hook. Bring the yarn **over** hook from **back** to **front**, catching the yarn with the hook and turning the hook slightly toward you to keep the yarn from slipping off. Draw the yarn through the slip knot *(Fig. 1)*.

Fig. 1

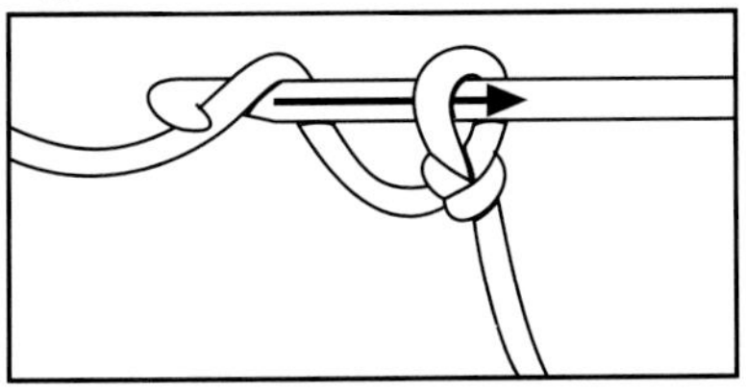

WORKING INTO THE CHAIN

When beginning a first row of crochet in a chain, always skip the first chain from the hook and work into the second chain from hook (for single crochet), third chain from hook (for half double crochet), or fourth chain from hook (for double crochet), etc. *(Fig. 2a)*.

Fig. 2a

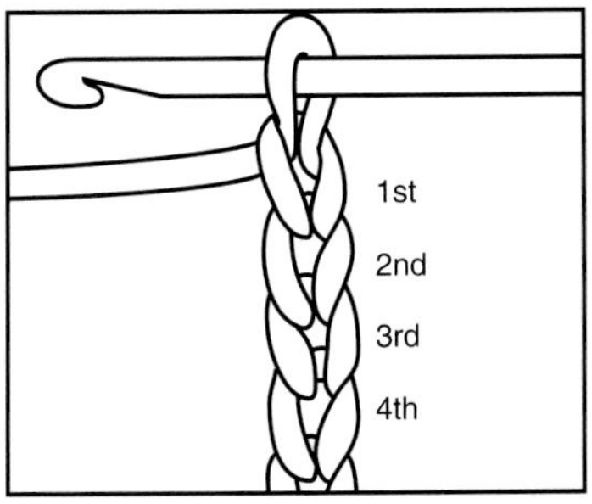

1st
2nd
3rd
4th

Method 1: Insert hook into back ridge of each chain indicated *(Fig. 2b)*.
Method 2: Insert hook under top two strands of each chain *(Fig. 2c)*.

Fig. 2b   **Fig. 2c**

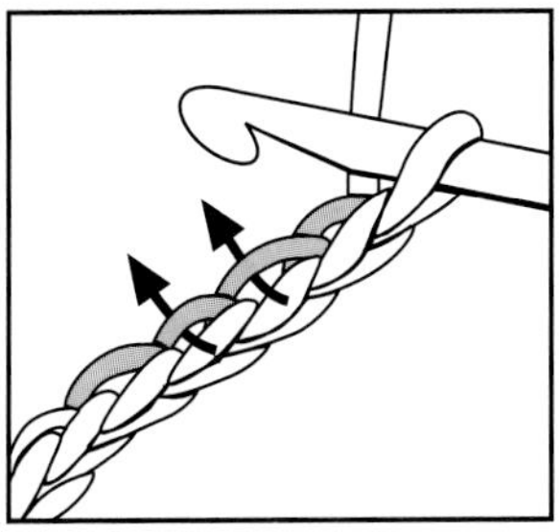

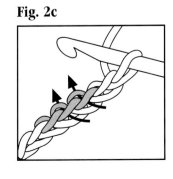

SLIP STITCH *(abbreviated slip st)*

This stitch is used to attach new yarn, to join work, or to move the yarn across a group of stitches without adding height. Insert hook in stitch or space indicated, YO and draw through stitch **and** loop on hook *(Fig. 3)*.

Fig. 3

SINGLE CROCHET *(abbreviated sc)*

Insert hook in stitch or space indicated, YO and pull up a loop, YO and draw through both loops on hook *(Fig. 4)*.

Fig. 4

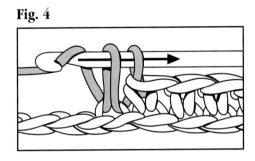

HALF DOUBLE CROCHET
(abbreviated hdc)

YO, insert hook in stitch or space indicated, YO and pull up a loop, YO and draw through all 3 loops on hook *(Fig. 5)*.

Fig. 5

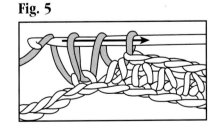

DOUBLE CROCHET (abbreviated dc)

YO, insert hook in stitch or space indicated, YO and pull up a loop (3 loops on hook), YO and draw through 2 loops on hook (*Fig. 6a*), YO and draw through remaining 2 loops on hook (*Fig. 6b*).

Fig. 6a

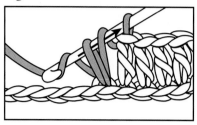

Fig. 6b

TREBLE CROCHET (abbreviated tr)

YO twice, insert hook in stitch or space indicated, YO and pull up a loop (4 loops on hook) (*Fig. 7a*), (YO and draw through 2 loops on hook) 3 times (*Fig. 7b*).

Fig. 7a   Fig. 7b

DOUBLE TREBLE CROCHET (abbreviated dtr)

YO 3 times, insert hook in stitch or space indicated, YO and pull up a loop (5 loops on hook) (*Fig. 8a*), (YO and draw through 2 loops on hook) 4 times (*Fig. 8b*).

Fig. 8a   Fig. 8b

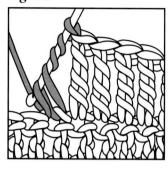
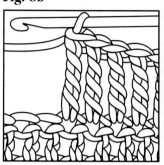

TRIPLE TREBLE CROCHET (abbreviated tr tr)

YO 4 times, insert hook in stitch or space indicated, YO and pull up a loop (6 loops on hook) (*Fig. 9a*), (YO and draw through 2 loops on hook) 5 times (*Fig. 9b*).

Fig. 9a   Fig. 9b

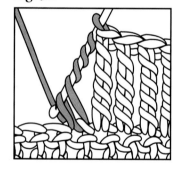

PATTERN STITCHES

POST STITCH

Work around post of stitch indicated, inserting hook in direction of arrow *(Fig. 10)*.

Fig. 10

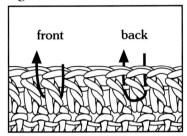

FRONT POST HALF DOUBLE CROCHET
(abbreviated FPhdc)

YO, insert hook from **front** to **back** around post of stitch indicated *(Fig. 10)*, YO and pull up a loop (3 loops on hook), YO and draw through all 3 loops on hook *(Fig. 11)*.

Fig. 11

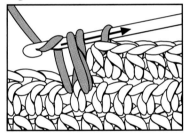

FRONT POST DOUBLE CROCHET
(abbreviated FPdc)

YO, insert hook from **front** to **back** around post of stitch indicated *(Fig. 10)*, YO and pull up a loop (3 loops on hook) *(Fig. 12)*, (YO and draw through 2 loops on hook) twice.

Fig. 12

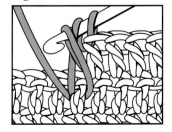

FRONT POST TREBLE CROCHET
(abbreviated FPtr)

YO twice, insert hook from **front** to **back** around post of stitch indicated *(Fig. 10)*, YO and pull up a loop (4 loops on hook) *(Fig. 13)*, (YO and draw through 2 loops on hook) 3 times.

Fig. 13

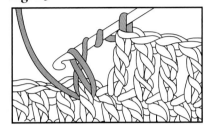

FRONT POST DOUBLE TREBLE CROCHET *(abbreviated FPdtr)*

YO 3 times, insert hook from **front** to **back** around post of stitch indicated *(Fig. 10)*, YO and pull up a loop (5 loops on hook) *(Fig. 14)*, (YO and draw through 2 loops on hook) 4 times.

Fig. 14

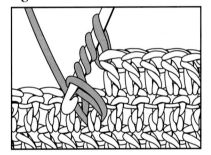

BACK POST DOUBLE CROCHET
(abbreviated BPdc)

YO, insert hook from **back** to **front** around post of stitch indicated *(Fig. 10, page 135)*, YO and pull up a loop (3 loops on hook) *(Fig. 15)*, (YO and draw through 2 loops on hook) twice.

Fig. 15

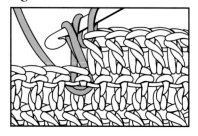

BACK POST TREBLE CROCHET
(abbreviated BPtr)

YO twice, insert hook from **back** to **front** around post of stitch indicated *(Fig. 10, page 135)*, YO and pull up a loop (4 loops on hook) *(Fig. 16)*, (YO and draw through 2 loops on hook) 3 times.

Fig. 16

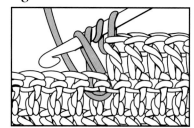

CLUSTER

A Cluster can be worked all in the same stitch or space *(Figs. 17a & b)*, **or** across several stitches *(Figs. 17c & d)*.

Fig. 17a

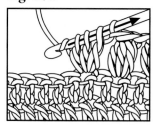

Fig. 17b

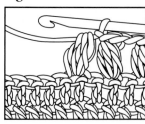

Fig. 17c

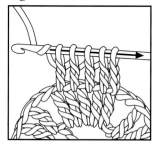

Fig. 17d

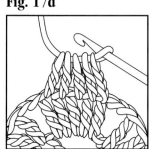

POPCORN

Work specified number of dc in stitch or space indicated, drop loop from hook, insert hook in first dc of dc group, hook dropped loop and draw through *(Figs. 18a & b)*.

Fig. 18a   **4-dc Popcorn**

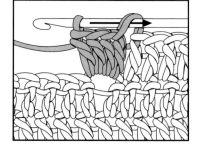

Fig. 18b   **5-dc Popcorn**

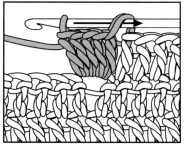

PUFF STITCH

★ YO, insert hook in stitch indicated, YO and pull up a loop even with loop on hook; repeat from ★ as many times as specified, YO and draw through all loops on hook *(Fig. 19)*.

Fig. 19

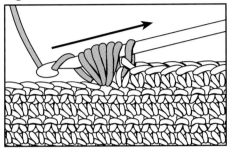

LONG STITCH

Work single crochet *(sc)*, double crochet *(dc)*, or treble crochet *(tr)*, inserting hook in stitch or space indicated in instructions *(Fig. 20)* and pulling up a loop even with loop on hook; complete stitch.

Fig. 20

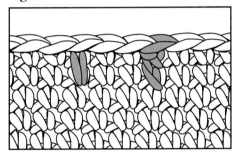

SPLIT LDC

YO, working around previous row, insert hook **through** post of LDC one row **below** next sc *(Fig. 21)*, YO and pull up a loop even with loop on hook, (YO and draw through 2 loops on hook) twice.

Fig. 21

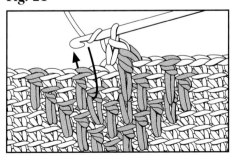

BEGINNING SPLIT TR

YO twice, insert hook from **back** to **front** in marked ch *(Fig. 22a)*, YO and pull up a loop, (YO and draw through 2 loops on hook) twice, YO twice, insert hook from **front** to **back** in next ch indicated *(Fig. 22b)*, YO and pull up a loop, (YO and draw through 2 loops on hook) twice, YO and draw through all 3 loops on hook.

Fig. 22a

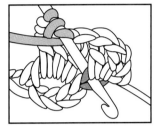

Fig. 22b

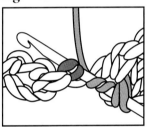

SPLIT TR

YO twice, working in **front** of last 3 dc made, insert hook from **back** to **front** in same ch as last Split tr made *(Fig. 23a)*, YO and pull up a loop, (YO and draw through 2 loops on hook) twice, YO twice, insert hook from **front** to **back** in next ch indicated *(Fig. 23b)*, YO and pull up a loop, (YO and draw through 2 loops on hook) twice, YO and draw through all 3 loops on hook.

Fig. 23a

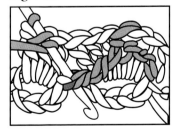

Fig. 23b

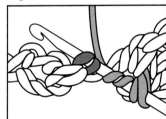

ENDING SPLIT TR

YO twice, working in **front** of last 3 dc made, insert hook from **back** to **front** in same ch as last Split tr made *(Fig. 24a)*, YO and pull up a loop, (YO and draw through 2 loops on hook) twice, YO twice, insert hook from **front** to **back** in first marked ch *(Fig. 24b)*, YO and pull up a loop, (YO and draw through 2 loops on hook) twice, YO and draw through all 3 loops on hook.

Fig. 24a

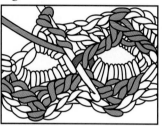

Fig. 24b

SPLIT TR CLUSTER

YO twice, working in **front** of last 3 dc made, insert hook from **back** to **front** in center of previous Split tr *(Fig. 25a)*, YO and pull up a loop, (YO and draw through 2 loops on hook) twice, YO twice, skip next 3 dc, insert hook from **front** to **back** in center of next Split tr *(Fig. 25b)*, YO and pull up a loop, (YO and draw through 2 loops on hook) twice, YO and draw through all 3 loops on hook.

Fig. 25a

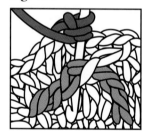

Fig. 25b

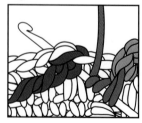

CABLE

Skip next 2 BPtr, work FPdtr around each of next 2 BPtr *(Fig. 26a)*, working in **front** of 2 FPdtr just made, work FPdtr around first skipped BPtr and around next skipped BPtr *(Fig. 26b)*.

Fig. 26a

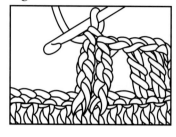

Fig. 26b

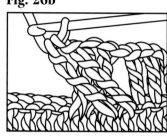

REVERSE SINGLE CROCHET

Working from **left** to **right**, ★ insert hook in st to right of hook *(Fig. 27a)*, YO and draw through, under, and to left of loop on hook (2 loops on hook) *(Fig. 27b)*, YO and draw through both loops on hook *(Fig. 27c)* (reverse sc made, *Fig. 27d*); repeat from ★ around.

Fig. 27a

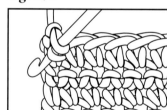

Fig. 27b

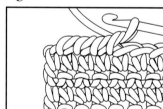

Fig. 27c

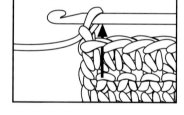

Fig. 27d

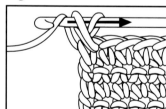

STITCHING TIPS

JOINING WITH SC

When instructed to join with sc, begin with a slip knot on hook. Insert hook in stitch or space indicated, YO and pull up a loop, yarn over and draw through both loops on hook.

BACK OR FRONT LOOP ONLY

Work only in loop(s) indicated by arrow *(Fig. 28)*.

Fig. 28

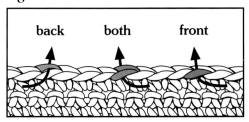

FREE LOOPS

After working in Back or Front Loops Only on a row or round, there will be a ridge of unused loops. These are called the free loops. Later, when instructed to work in the free loops of the same row or round, work in these loops *(Fig. 29a)*.
When instructed to work in a free loop of a beginning chain, work in loop indicated by arrow *(Fig. 29b)*.

Fig. 29a

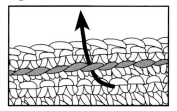

Fig. 29b

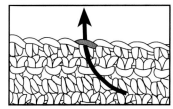

ADDING ON DC

When instructed to add on dc at the end of a row, YO, insert hook into base of last dc made *(Fig. 30)*, YO and pull up a loop, YO and draw through one loop on hook, (YO and draw through 2 loops on hook) twice. Repeat as many times as instructed.

Fig. 30

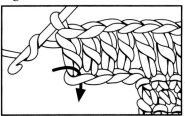

CHANGING COLORS

Work the last stitch to within one step of completion, hook new yarn *(Fig. 31a)* and draw through loops on hook. Cut old yarn and work over both ends unless otherwise specified.
When working in rounds, drop old yarn; using new yarn, join with slip stitch to first stitch *(Fig. 31b)*.

Fig. 31a

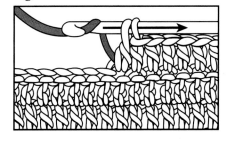

Fig. 31b

NO-SEW JOINING

Hold Squares, Motifs, or Strips with **wrong** sides together. Slip st or sc into space as indicated *(Fig. 32)*.

Fig. 32

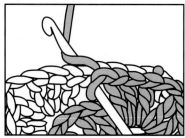

MARKERS

Markers are used to help distinguish the beginning of each round being worked. Place a 2" scrap piece of yarn before the first stitch of each round, moving marker after each round is complete.

WORKING IN SPACE BEFORE STITCH

When instructed to work in space **before** a stitch or in spaces **between** stitches, insert hook in space indicated by arrow *(Fig. 33)*.

Fig. 33

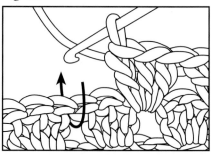

WEAVING IN YARN ENDS

Good finishing techniques make a big difference in the quality of any crocheted piece. Make a habit of weaving in loose ends as you work. **Never** tie a knot in your yarn. They may poke through to the right side and will sometimes come untied and unravel. Weaving in the ends gives a much better result. Thread a yarn needle with the yarn end. With **wrong** side facing, weave the needle through several stitches, then reverse the direction and weave it back through several more stitches. When the end is secure, clip the yarn off close to your work.

You may also hide your ends as you work by crocheting over them for several inches to secure, then weave in opposite direction; clip the remaining lengths off close to your work. Always check your work to be sure the yarn ends do not show on the right side.

FINISHING

WEAVING

With **wrong** sides facing, place pieces to be woven together side by side on a flat surface; sew through both pieces once to secure the beginning of the seam, leaving an ample yarn end to weave in later. Insert needle from **right** to **left** through back strand (just below top loop) of first st on both pieces *(Fig. 34a)*. Bring the needle around and insert it from **right** to **left**, through the **next** strand on both pieces.
Repeat along the edge, being careful to match stitches.

Fig. 34a wrong side

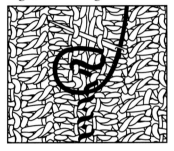

Fig. 34b right side

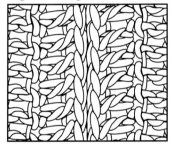

WHIPSTITCH

With **wrong** sides together and beginning in corner stitch, sew through both pieces once to secure the beginning of the seam, leaving an ample yarn end to weave in later. Insert needle from **front** to **back** through **inside** loops of **each** piece *(Fig. 35a)* **or** through **both** loops *(Fig. 35b)*. Bring needle around and insert it from **front** to **back** through the next loops of **both** pieces. Continue in this manner across to corner, keeping the sewing yarn fairly loose.

Fig. 35a

Fig. 35b

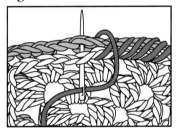

FRINGE

Cut a piece of cardboard 8" wide and ½" longer than desired fringe. Wind the yarn **loosely** and **evenly** around the length of the cardboard until the card is filled, then cut across one end; repeat as needed. Align the number of strands desired and fold in half.

With **wrong** side facing and using a crochet hook, draw the folded end up through a stitch, row, or loop, and pull the loose ends through the folded end *(Figs. 36a & b)*; draw the knot up **tightly** *(Figs. 36c & d)*. Repeat, spacing as specified. Lay flat on a hard surface and trim the ends.

Fig. 36a

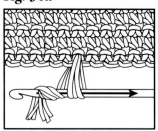

Fig. 36b

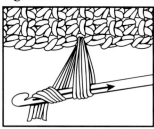

Fig. 36c

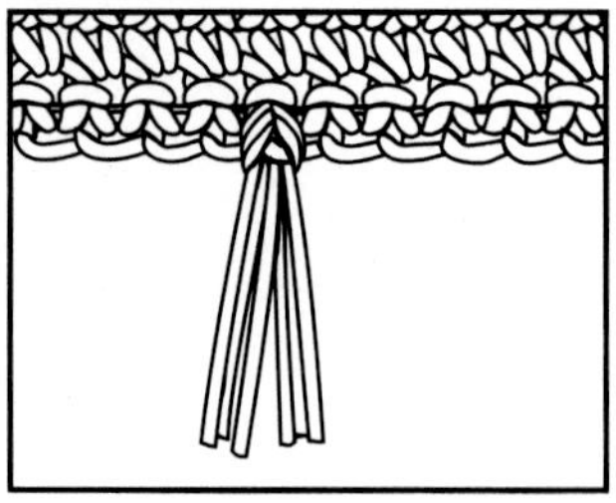

Fig. 36d

TASSEL

Cut a piece of cardboard 3" wide and as long as you want your finished tassel to be. Wind a double strand of yarn around the cardboard approximately 12 times. Cut an 18" length of yarn and insert it under all of the strands at the top of the cardboard; pull up **tightly** and tie securely. Leave the yarn ends long enough to attach the tassel. Cut the yarn at the opposite end of the cardboard and then remove it *(Fig. 37a)*. Cut a 6" length of yarn and wrap it **tightly** around the tassel twice, 1" below the top *(Fig. 37b)*; tie securely. Trim the ends.

Fig. 37a

Fig. 37b

credits

To Magna IV Color Imaging of Little Rock, Arkansas, we say thank you for the superb color reproduction and excellent pre-press preparation.

We want to especially thank photographers Ken West, Larry Pennington, Mark Mathews, and Karen Shirey of Peerless Photography, Little Rock, Arkansas, and Jerry R. Davis of Jerry Davis Photography, Little Rock, Arkansas, for their time, patience, and excellent work.

We would like to extend a special word of thanks to the talented designers who created the lovely projects in this book:

Eleanor Albano: *Victorian Gem*, page 16
Alexander-Stratton: *Chain of Hearts*, page 22; *Lacy Lullaby*, page 38; *Brown-Eyed Susans*, page 96; *Bow Ties*, page 106; and *Appealing Pineapples*, page 118
Judy Bolin: *Granny Stripes*, page 94, and *Radiant Mums*, page 102
Delores Franks: *Baby's Choice*, page 82
Nancy Fuller: *Rustic Log Cabin*, page 6, and *Forest Dream*, page 108
Sue Galucki: *Snow Crystals*, page 126
Anne Halliday: *Snowball Blanket*, page 10; *Pretty Pattern*, page 44; *Dancing Daffodils*, page 46; *Seashell Baskets*, page 80; *Ocean Waves*, page 84; *Shells in a Net*, page 88; and *Bandanna Blocks*, page 98
Jan Hatfield: *Mile-A-Minute Blues*, page 28; *Earth Awakens*, page 30; *Old-Time Charm*, page 52; *Dreamy Shells*, page 60; *Dad's Comfy Wrap*, page 64; and *Summer Sunrise*, page 78
Terry Kimbrough: *Timeless Tulips*, page 40; *United in Love*, page 62; *Rock-A-Bye Roses*, page 66; and *Decked with Holly*, page 128
Ann Kirtley: *Lilac Garden*, page 54, and *Elegance for Mother*, page 56
Jennine Korejko: *Spring Splendor*, page 42, and *Light and Lacy*, page 50
Patricia Kristoffersen: *Rosy Trellis*, page 68
Melissa Leapman: *Star-Spangled Salute*, page 76, and *Buffalo Plaid*, page 122
Debra Nettles: *Easter Eggs*, page 32
Carole Prior: *Garnet Fans*, page 8; *Granny's Mums*, page 12; *American Ripple*, page 74; *Rippling Effects*, page 86; *Busy Lizzies*, page 90; *Blue Ribbon Winner*, page 104; *Handsome Ripple*, page 112; *Falling Leaves*, page 114; *Indian Summer*, page 116; and *Christmas Eve*, page 124
C. A. Riley: *Sweet Rainbow*, page 34
Betty Scharf: *Pretty Pillowghan*, page 18
Mary Ann Sipes: *Valentine Wrap*, page 20; *Four-Leaf Clovers*, page 26; and *Primary Rainbow,* page 92